Ornamental Design
Using Adobe® Illustrator®

David T. Curtis

Ornamental Design
Using Adobe® Illustrator®

by David T. Curtis

Adobe, the Adobe logo, Adobe Illustrator, the Adobe Illustrator logo, Adobe InDesign, Adobe Photoshop and Creative Cloud are either registered trademarks or trademarks of Adobe Systems Incorporated in the United States and/or other countries.

All other trademarks are property of their respective owners.

While every precaution has been taken in the preparation of this book, the author assumes no responsibility for errors or omissions, or for damages resulting from the use of the information contained herein.

THIS PRODUCT IS NOT AUTHORIZED, ENDORSED OR SPONSORED BY ADOBE SYSTEMS INCORPORATED, PUBLISHER OF ADOBE® ILLUSTRATOR®

Adobe product screenshot(s) reprinted with permission from Adobe Systems Incorporated.

ISBN-13: 978-1981325184
ISBN-10: 1981325182

First Edition

Contents

Introduction

Getting Started

This book is a collection of design techniques aimed at using ADOBE® ILLUSTRATOR® CC to create designs with classic ornamental style. Applying a classic ornamental style can make your designs look elegant and valuable.

Design Software

This book is written with the assumption that the user is familiar with ADOBE® ILLUSTRATOR® CC. You will need ADOBE® ILLUSTRATOR® CC to complete the examples shown in this book. Earlier versions of ADOBE® ILLUSTRATOR® including CS-6 will probably work fine, however the earlier versions may have a slightly different user interface.

Planning Ahead

Producing a classic ornamental design requires planning. You need to know sizes and printing parameters before creating your artwork. Line-widths and spacing are critical, and can become problematic if they need to be scaled and stretched to fit different document sizes. Make sure you know what size document you are producing before you get started. It is also important to know some technical printing parameters, like the minimum printable line width, to make sure your document is designed properly.

Ink colors are also import for intricate ornamental design. You generally want to use spot colors rather than process colors, and avoid setting up your file in a way that will generate halftone dots when printed.

Support Website

To download the files for all of the examples in this book, please go to:

DavidTCurtis.wixsite.com/OrnamentalDesign

Email

To contact the author of this book, send an email to:

OrnamentalDesignAI@gmail.com

Design Templates

ADOBE® ILLUSTRATOR® makes it easy to setup precise templates assuring your design will be printed at the right size and dimension. Be sure to always start your project with the correct document size, and use guides for placing key items in the proper locations. Your design will not look valuable if the design elements are not centered precisely or properly aligned. Guides are simply reference lines that appear on the screen in ADOBE® ILLUSTRATOR®, but are invisible when printed or exported. To get started, we will create a design template for a certificate style design on U.S. letter size paper with a half-inch margin on all four sides. A sketch of the layout, like the one below, will make it faster and easier to create an accurate template.

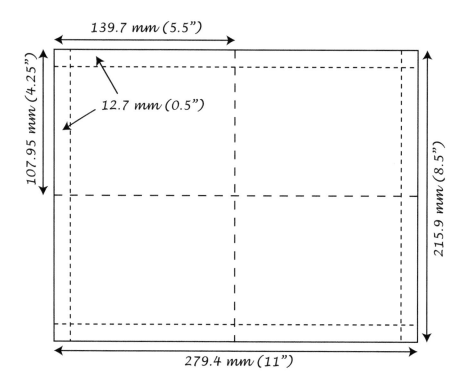

EXAMPLE 1: Create "EX01 Letter Size Template" File

In ADOBE® ILLUSTRATOR®, select: *File->New* from the top menu bar and then setup the new document with the following parameters as shown below:

Name: **EX01 Letter Size Template**
Number of Artboards: **1**
Size: **Letter** (or Custom)
Units: **Millimeters**
Width: **279.4 mm**
Height: **215.9 mm**
Orientation: **Landscape (Horizontal)**
Bleed: **0 mm** (for all four options: Top, Bottom…)
Color Mode: **CMYK**
Raster Effects: **High (300ppi)**
Preview Mode: **Default**

(New Version)

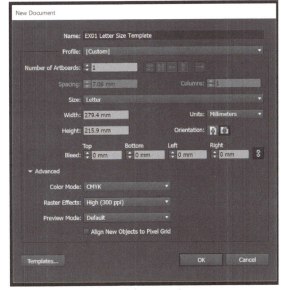

(Old Version)

Tip: Recent updates to the New Document dialogue box might look different than the example shown here. If the New Document dialogue box does not show the same settings, look for a button labeled: "More Settings".

I recommend using the "Layout" workspace for this exercise. You can switch to the "Layout" workspace by selecting: *Window->Workspace->Layout* from the top menu bar. You will also need the rulers turned on. To turn on the rulers, select: *View->Rulers->Show Rulers* from the top menu bar.

Your ADOBE® ILLUSTRATOR® workspace should now look similar to the following:

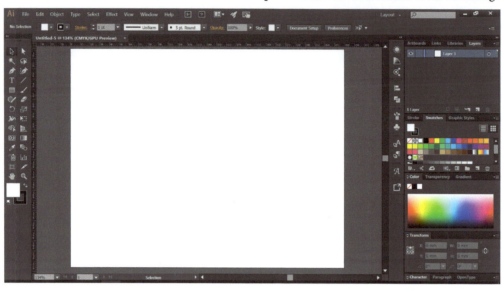

Create a Layer for Your Guides

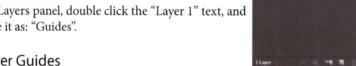

Tip: If you cannot find the Layers panel, select *Window->Layers* in the menu, or press *F7*.

1   In the Layers panel, double click the "Layer 1" text, and rename it as: "Guides".

Add Center Guides

Center guides will allow you to position design elements in precise alignment with the center of the document.

Tip: If you do not see the rulers, select: *View->Rulers->Show Rulers* in the top menu bar.

2   Click on the horizontal ruler (x-axis), and drag downward to create a horizontal guide line.

IMPORTANT! Before working with guides make sure the guides are not locked. Select: *View->Guides->Unlock Guides* from the top menu bar if you cannot select and move the guides.

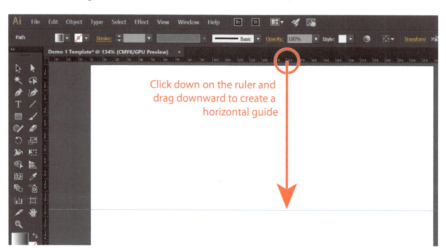

Click down on the ruler and drag downward to create a horizontal guide

3   Now use the Transform panel to position the guide exactly in the center of the page. First, make sure the guide is selected. If not, click on the Selection Tool or press V on the keyboard. Then, click on the guide.

In the Transform panel, set the Reference Point to the center block. This will allow you to position the guide in reference to its center. After you have set the reference point enter the following values into the transform panel to position the guide in the center of the page:

Tip: Make sure to use the selection tool 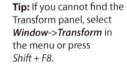 when selecting guides and transforming them.

Tip: If you cannot find the Transform panel, select *Window->Transform* in the menu or press *Shift + F8*.

Tip: The Transform panel has a built-in calculator. Just type in the math expression and ADOBE® ILLUSTRATOR® will calculate it for you. If you want to move something down 2mm, click on the Y value in the textbox and add "+2mm" on to the end of the value that is already there.

Set the Reference Point to the center block

Set the X-coordinate to the center point (half the width)

Set the Width to the width of the page

Set the Y-coordinate to the center point (half the height)

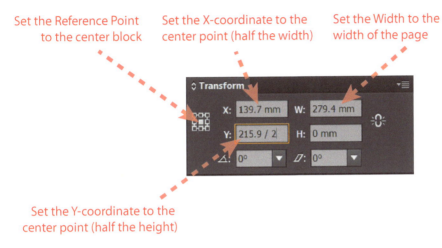

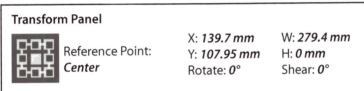

Transform Panel

Reference Point: *Center*

X: *139.7 mm*
Y: *107.95 mm*
Rotate: *0°*

W: *279.4 mm*
H: *0 mm*
Shear: *0°*

4   Click on the vertical ruler (y-axis), and drag to the left to create a vertical guide line.

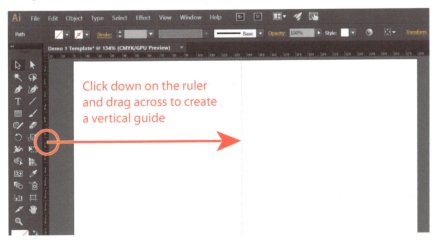

Click down on the ruler and drag across to create a vertical guide

5   With the guide selected, use the transform panel to position it exactly in the center of the page.

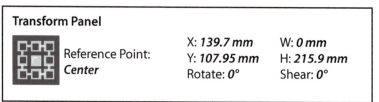

Transform Panel

Reference Point: *Center*

X: *139.7 mm*   W: *0 mm*
Y: *107.95 mm*   H: *215.9 mm*
Rotate: *0°*   Shear: *0°*

You should now have two guides forming a cross-hair in the center of the page as shown below:

Add Margin Guides

Now we need to create guides for the borders of our document that are 12.7 mm (1/2 inch) from the edge of the page.

6   To create the top border guide, select the horizontal center guide, and then copy and paste it. You can use the Edit menu, or type the copy and paste key commands. Then, place the new guide in the correct position using the Transform Panel with the following:

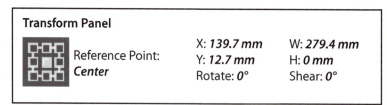

Transform Panel

Reference Point: *Center*

X: *139.7 mm*   W: *279.4 mm*
Y: *12.7 mm*   H: *0 mm*
Rotate: *0°*   Shear: *0°*

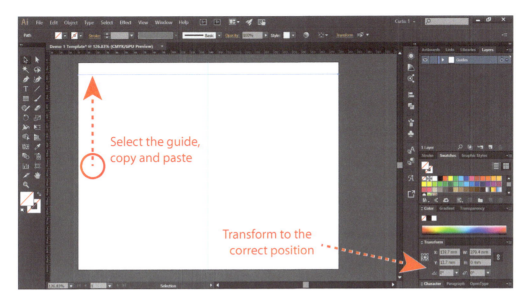

Select the guide, copy and paste

Transform to the correct position

7 Copy, paste and transform again to create the bottom guide line. Use the following to transform the bottom guide to the correct position:

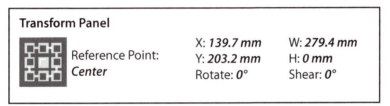

Transform Panel

Reference Point: *Center*

X: *139.7 mm*
Y: *203.2 mm*
Rotate: *0°*

W: *279.4 mm*
H: *0 mm*
Shear: *0°*

8 Repeat the copy, paste, transform process using the vertical center guide to create the left and right border guide lines.

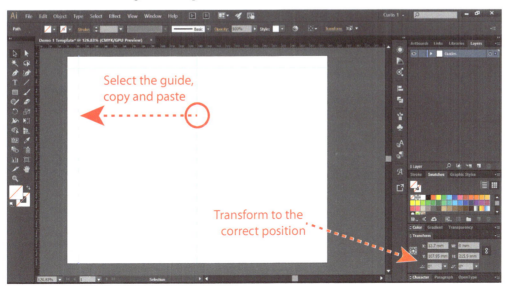

Select the guide, copy and paste

Transform to the correct position

Left border guide transform position:

Transform Panel

Reference Point: *Center*

X: *12.7 mm*
Y: *107.95 mm*
Rotate: *0°*

W: *0 mm*
H: *215.9 mm*
Shear: *0°*

Right border guide transform position

Transform Panel

Reference Point: *Center*

X: *266.7 mm*
Y: *107.95 mm*
Rotate: *0°*

W: *0 mm*
H: *215.9 mm*
Shear: *0°*

After all the guides have been correctly positioned, your page should look similar to below:

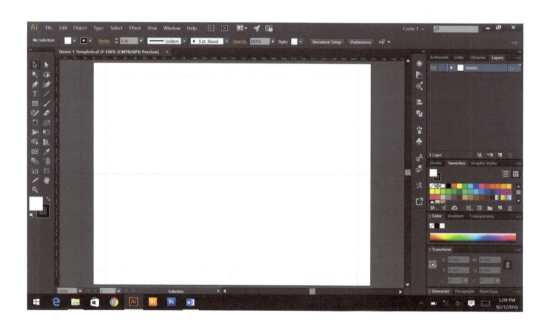

Lock Down the Guides

Now, you are ready to lock down the guides.

9   In the Layers panel, click on the box next to the small eye so that a lock appears in the box (see picture below). This locks the guides in their position, and prevents you from accidentally moving them.

10   Next, make a new layer by clicking the Create New Layer button on the Layers Panel. You can leave it named "Layer 2". Layer 2 will be the layer that you use to start your artwork. Setting up this layer in the template will help users avoid creating artwork on the Guides layer after a new document is created from this template.

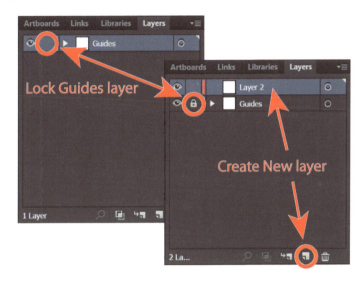

Tip: The column to the right of the eye icon in the Layers panel is called the "Edit Column". Click on the Edit Column next to the layer name to "lock" the items in that layer. Locking the items means that you cannot edit or move them. This is useful when you want prevent yourself from inadvertently selecting or moving items in a complex piece of artwork.

Tip: You can also lock selected items or groups by choosing: *Object->Lock->Selection*.

Simplify the Ink Palette

One of the most common mistakes designers make when creating designs for print is using the wrong ink color swatches. I recommend setting up your template with a minimal set of color swatches, and only add color swatches for inks you intend to use when the document is printed.

The minimum color swatches are: None, Registration, White and Black. The "None" color swatch is basically the same as clear. There is a difference between "None" and "White". "None" is transparent and will not cover up items behind it. Items colored "White" are opaque and will cover up items behind it.

11 On the Swatches panel, click on the drop drown menu and select "Select All Unused". Then delete all of the unused swatches by clicking on the trashcan icon.

12 Next, click on the folder labeled "Grays" and delete that as well.

13 Select "Small List View" from the drop down menu, and you should only see the bare minimum color swatches.

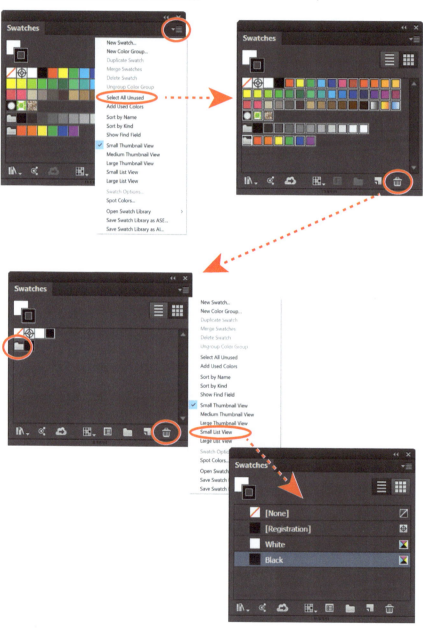

Ready to Save the Template

You are now finished and ready to save the template.

14   Select **File->Save as Template...** from the top menu.

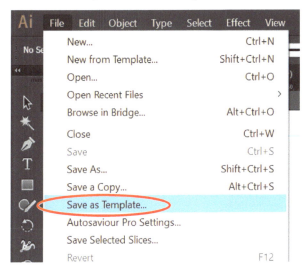

15   Filename: "EX01 Letter Size Template".

EXAMPLE 2: Create "EX02 Half Inch Border Template"

The following is an example of how to create a document border with masks that can be filled with various patterns.

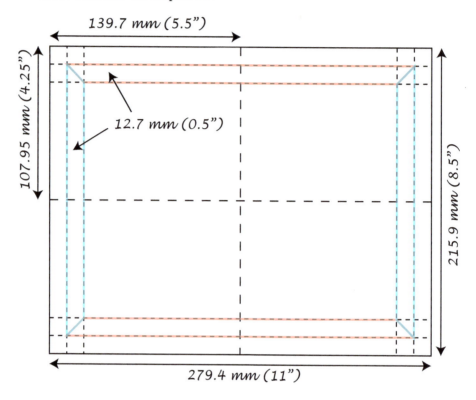

File Setup

1   First, we will continue from the previous EX01 Letter Size Template. You can continue from the previous example or download the EX01 Letter Size file from the website: *DavidTCurtis.wixsite.com/OrnamentalDesign*

2   If you want to start by loading the template from the previous example, select **File->New From Template...** from the top menu bar.

Guides

Next, we will setup the guides.

1   Select the "Guides" layer and unlock it.

2   Using the Selection Tool(▷), select the top guide.

IMPORTANT! Before working with guides make sure the guides are not locked. Select: *View->Guides->Unlock Guides* from the top menu bar if you cannot select and move the guides.

3   Select *Object->Transform->Move* from the top menu bar.

4   In the Move Dialogue, input the following:
Horizontal: 0 mm
Vertical: 12.7 mm
Select the Copy button.

5   Select the bottom guide.

6   Select *Object->Transform->Move* from the top menu bar.

7   In the Move Dialogue, input the following:
Horizontal: 0 mm
Vertical: -12.7 mm
Select the Copy button

    .

8   Select the left guide.

9   Select *Object->Transform->Move* from the top menu bar.

10 In the Move Dialogue, input the following:
Horizontal: 12.7 mm
Vertical: 0 mm
Select the Copy button.

11 Select the right guide.

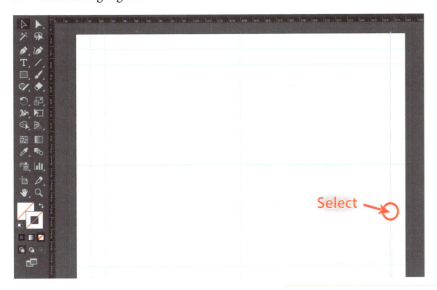

12 Select *Object->Transform->Move* from the top menu bar.

13 In the Move Dialogue, input the following:
    Horizontal: 0 mm
    Vertical: -12.7 mm
    Select the Copy button.

14 Lock the "Guides Layer".

Draw Top Border Mask

Next, we will create the top border mask.

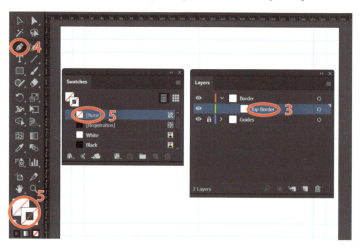

1 Rename "Layer 2" as "Border".

2 With the "Border" layer selected, click on the Create New Sublayer button (▣) at the bottom of the Layers panel.

3 Rename new sublayer as "Top Border".

4 Select the Pen Tool (🖊).

5 Set the Stroke Color to [None], and the Fill to [None].

6 Make sure Snap to Point option is on. (There should be a check mark next to menu item View->Snap to Point).

7 Click on the intersection of the top and left guides as shown below. A small text pop-up should say "intersect" when the pointer is hovering over the correct location.

Click

8   Click on the other points shown below, and then back on the top left intersection to complete the shape.

9   Hide the "Top Border" sublayer.

Draw Bottom Border Mask

Next, we will create the bottom border mask.

10   Select the "Border" layer and create a new sublayer.

11   Rename the new sublayer as, "Bottom Border".

12   Select the Pen Tool ().

13   Click on the points shown below to complete the shape.

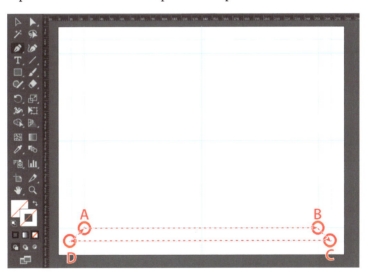

14   Hide the "Bottom Border" sublayer.

Draw Left Border Mask

Next, we will create the left border mask.

15   Select the "Border" layer and create a new
      sublayer.

16   Rename the new sublayer as, "Left Border".

17   Select the Pen Tool ().

18   Click on the points shown below to complete the shape.

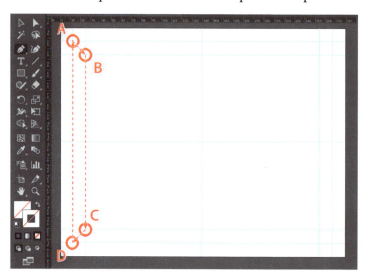

19   Hide the "Left Border" sublayer.

Draw Right Border Mask

Next, we will create the right border mask.

20   Select the "Border" layer and create a new sublayer.

21   Rename the new sublayer as, "Right Border".

22 Select the Pen Tool (![pen tool icon]).

23 Click on the points shown below to complete the shape.

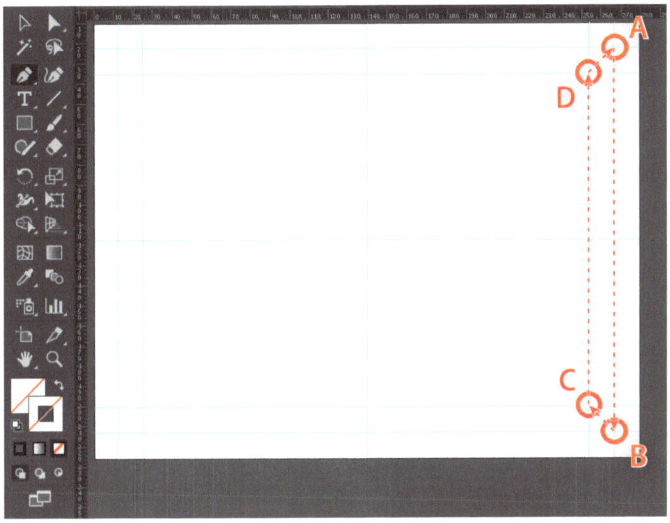

24 Show all the border sublayers.

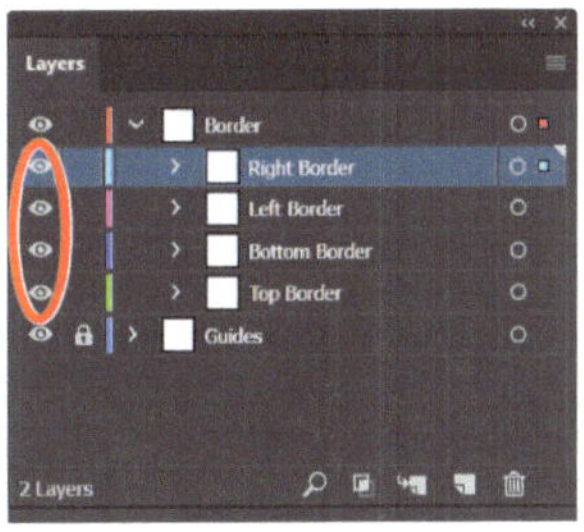

Finishing Up

Next, we will save the template for later use.

25 Select the "Border" layer and create a new sublayer named, "Blend Keys".

26 Verify that the Layers are set up correctly:

Layers:

- Border
  - Blend Keys
  - Top Border
  - Left Border
  - Bottom Border
  - Right Border
- Guides

27 Select ***File->Save as Template...***

28 Filename: "EX2 Half Inch Border Template".

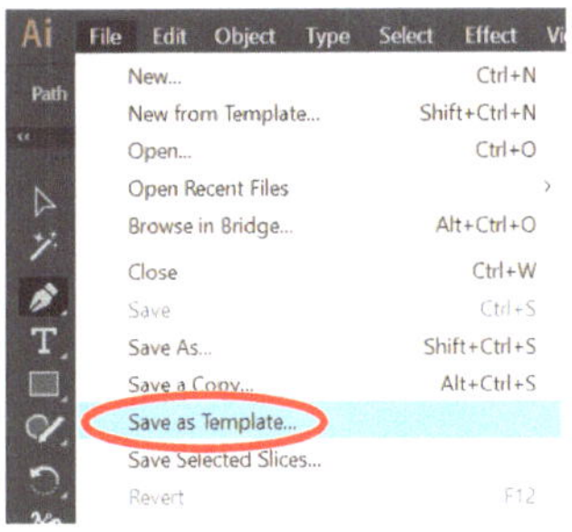

You can experiment with different fill patterns by selecting ***Window->Swatch Libraries->Patterns...***

Vector Design Essentials

The examples throughout this section show how you can enhance a piece of text using drop shadows, contour lines and fill patterns. These techniques can be applied to almost any type of shape, design or logo.

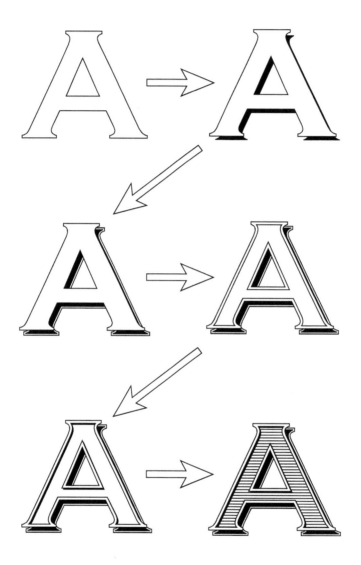

EXAMPLE 3: Contoured Drop Shadow

The following contoured shadow design can be easily applied to most type fonts. If you look closely at other documents, you may find this technique used in certificates and other documents with intrinsic value.

This design is created using a dark drop-shadow under an open-face font. The key to adding sophistication to the design is creating a thin white outline adjacent to the dark drop-shadow. The thin white outline next to a dark solid drop-shadow is difficult to reproduce without a high resolution output device. In this example, we will use a 0.25pt outline and gap. A thinner line weight and gap are feasible, but be sure to check with the printer to find out the minimum line weight and gap they are able to reliably print.

Note: An Open-Face Font has an outline, and a Closed-Face Font is filled in:
OPEN FACE
CLOSED FACE

Actual Size

Enlarged

Layer 1	*Layer 2*	*Layer 3*
Face Text	*Drop Shadow*	*Drop Shadow Outline*
Fill: White	*Fill: Black*	*Fill: White*
Stroke: Black	*Stroke: White*	*Stroke: Black*
Stroke Weight: 0.25pt	*Stroke Weight: 0.25pt*	*Stroke Weight: 0.25pt*
Align Stroke to Center	*Align Stroke to Inside*	*Align Stroke to Outside*

To get started we will use the template from Exercise 1. Select the menu item: *File->New from Template*, and select the "EX01 Letter Size Template" file in the dialog box. You can also download the file from: *DavidTCurtis.wixsite.com/OrnamentalDesign*

Using our template from the previous exercise, we will size and position our text in the top center of the page like shown in the figure below.

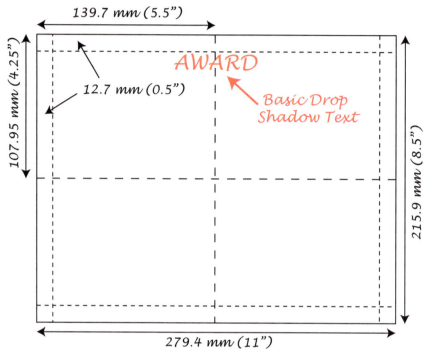

Layer Setup

ADOBE® ILLUSTRATOR® allows you to organize your artwork using layers. Keeping design elements separated and organized in layers is critical for complex security designs.

Note: It is important to keep your layers and sublayers organized and labeled when creating ornamental designs. This will make things much easier as you build a complex document.

1   Rename "Layer 2" as "Award Text"

2   With the "Award Text" layer selected, click on the Create New Sublayer button (⬚) at the bottom of the Layers panel.

3   Select the "Award Text" layer again and add a two more sublayers. Make sure you select the "Award Text" layer each time before creating the sublayers or you will create nested sublayers.

Correct   **Wrong**

4 Rename the sublayers in the following order:
   Layers:
   > Award Text
   >> Face Text
   >> Drop Shadow
   >> Drop Shadow Outline
   > Guides

Tip: You can click and drag the sublayers to place them in the correct order.

Face Text
We will start with Sublayer 1: "Face Text".

1 Select the "Face Text" sublayer.

2 Tool setup: Select the Type Tool (T) in the tool bar.
   Set the font to "Copperplate Gothic Bold", Size: 48pt
   Set the alignment to "Align Center"

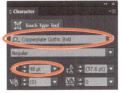

3 Click somewhere near the top center of the template, and type "AWARD" in all caps. (We will move the text into the correct position in step 6.)

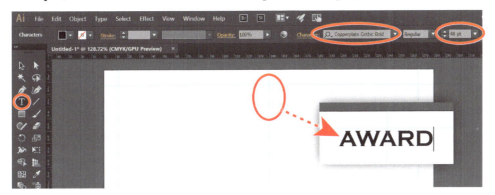

4 Switch to the Selection Tool (▶) then, select *Type->Create Outlines* from the top Menu Bar.

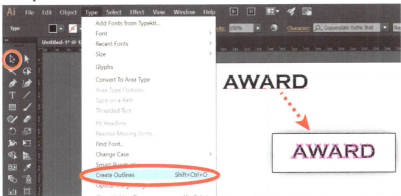

Tip: The origin is the location of (0,0) on the x,y axis of the page. You can set the origin anywhere on the page. This makes it easy to position artwork without doing any math. The default location for the origin is at the top-left of the page.

You can change the location of the origin by clicking down on the square located where the horizontal and vertical rulers meet, and then dragging the origin to a new location on the page.

Tip: If you cannot find the Stroke Panel, select: *Window->Stroke* from the top menu bar.

5   Set the origin to the intersection of the top center guides.

6   Make sure the AWARD text is selected and use the Transform Panel to move the AWARD text to (0,0).

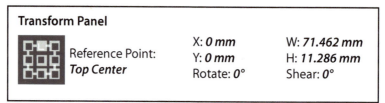

7   In the Stroke Panel, set the Stroke Weight to 0.25pt You can type the number or select it from the drop-down menu.

8   Set the stroke color to Black, and set the Fill to White.

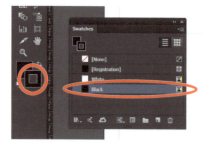
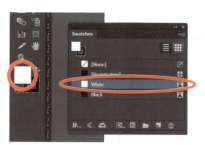

Drop Shadow

Next, we will setup Sublayer 2: "Drop Shadow".

1   Select the AWARD text we just created, and then select **Edit->Copy** form the menu.

Tip: Click the eye icon next to the layer name to hide the layer. This helps to isolate the layers you need to edit. When you hide a layer, nothing happens to the items in the layer. You just can't see the items until you choose to show the layer again.

2   Hide the "Face Text" sublayer by clicking on the eye icon.

3   Click on the "Drop Shadow" sublayer.

4   Select **Edit->Paste In Place** from the menu.

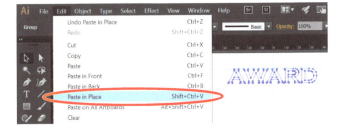

Note: Paste in Place will preserve the object coordinates when pasting an item that has been copied.
Using "Paste" instead of "Paste in Place" will place the items in the center of the current position of the screen viewport.

5   Set the drop shadow Fill to Black.

6   Set the Stroke Weight to 0.25 pt. Select Align Stroke to Inside and set the stroke color swatch to White.

Note: Align Stroke: You can choose to align the stroke to the center (default), inside or outside of the edges of an outline. However, this option is only available on objects with a closed path like a circle or polygon. If the Align Stroke option is disabled, then the object path needs to be closed or the item or text may need to be converted to outlines.

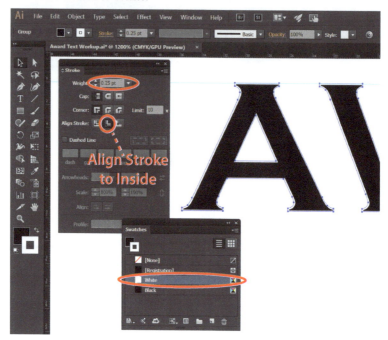

7   Use the Transform Panel to move the drop shadow down 0.5 mm, and to the right 0.5 mm.

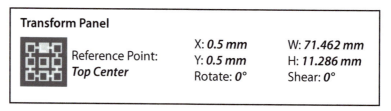

Transform Panel			
Reference Point: **Top Center**	X: **0.5 mm** Y: **0.5 mm** Rotate: **0°**	W: **71.462 mm** H: **11.286 mm** Shear: **0°**	

8   Show the "Face Text" sublayer by clicking on the eye icon, and zoom in to check your drop shadow.

Drop Shadow Outline
Finally, we will create Sublayer 3: "Drop Shadow Outline"

1   Hide the "Face Text" sublayer.

2   Select the Drop Shadow text. You can set the selection by clicking on the object or you can select all of the items in a layer by clicking on the small circle to the right of the layer name in the Layers Panel.

3   Select *Edit->Copy* form the menu.

Tip: You can also hide selected items or groups by choosing: *Object->Hide->Selection*. To show any and all hidden items select: *Object->Show All*.

4   Hide the "Drop Shadow" sublayer by clicking on the eye icon.

5   Click on the "Drop Shadow Outline" sublayer.

6   Select *Edit->Paste In Place* from the menu.

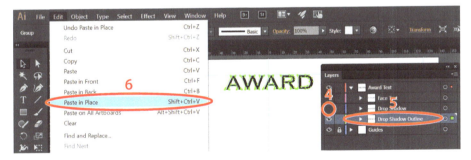

7   Set the Fill to [None].

8   Set the Stroke Weight to 0.25pt. Select Align Stroke to Outside and set the
    stroke color swatch to Black

9   Show all the sublayers, and you are finished. Save this file for later use.

EXAMPLE 4: Text Face Bezel

The following is an example of how to add a bezel edge to the face of your text. It will work for most fonts, but be sure to convert the type to outlines before using this method. In this example we will continue from the previous one, because this bezel technique combined with the drop shadow works very well to add an elegant ornate look to ordinary text.

Actual Size

Enlarged

Layer 1
Bezel Outline
Fill: None
Stroke: Black
Stroke Weight: 0.25pt
Align Stroke to Center

Layer 2
Bezel Shadow
Fill: Black
Stroke: None

Start with Drop Shadow Text

To get started, you can continue from the previous Contoured Drop Shadow Example, or download the startup file (*EX04 Text Face Bezel Start.ai*) from: *DavidTCurtis.wixsite.com/OrnamentalDesign*

Tip: If you cannot find the Layers panel, select *Window > Layers* in the menu or press *F7.*

If you see only two layers in the Layers Panel, click on the dropdown arrow next to the layer named, "Award Text".

Bezel Outline

First, we will setup the sublayers and create the bezel outline.

1   Select the "Award Text" Layer.

2   Create three new sublayers.

Make 3 Sublayers

3   Rename the sublayers in the following order:

         Layers:

                 Award Text
                     Bezel Outline
                     Bezel Shadow
                     Bezel Fill
                     Face Text
                     Drop Shadow
                     Drop Shadow Outline
             Guides

4   Select the Face Text. You can set the selection by clicking on the object or you can select all of the items in a layer by clicking on the small circle to the right of the layer name in the Layers Panel.

5   Select *Object->Path->Offset Path...*

6   Set the Offset Path settings to:
Offset: **-0.3mm**
Joins: **Miter** (Default)
Miter Limit: **4** (Default)
Select the OK Button.

Note: The "Offset Path" function will create a contour line around the outside of the artwork if you use a positive number, and it will create a contour line around the inside if you use a negative number.

7   Select *Edit->Cut.*

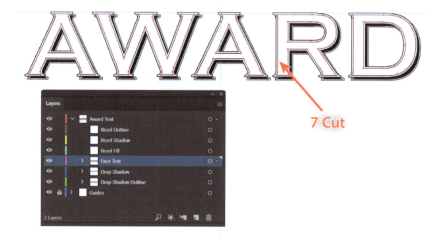

8   Hide the "Face Text", "Drop Shadow" and "Drop Shadow Outline" sublayers.

9   Select "Bezel Outline" sublayer.

10   Select *Edit->Paste in Place.*

11   Select *Object->Compound Path->Make.*

12   Set the Fill to [None].

Bezel Shadow

Next, we will create the bezel shadow.

1   With the Bezel Outline still selected, Select **Edit->Copy**.

2   Hide the "Bezel Outline" sublayer.

3   Select the "Bezel Shadow" sublayer.

4   Select **Edit->Paste in Place.**

5   Select **Object->Transform->Move.**

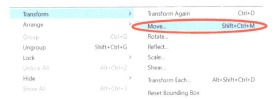

Tip: The Move dialogue box is similar to the Transform panel. The Move dialogue box is useful for moving items a specific distance and at an angle.

6   In the Move Dialogue, input the following:

Distance: **0.2mm**
Angle: **-45**
Then select the **Copy** button.

The copy button will make a copy that has been moved and leave the old one in place.

7   Select everything in the "Bezel Shadow" sublayer by clicking on the circle to the right of the sublayer name in the Layers Panel.

Tip: You can open the Pathfinder Panel by selecting: *Window->Pathfinder* in the top menu bar.

You can also select: *Effect->Pathfinder->Subtract* to do the same thing as Minus Front.

8   Click on the Shape Mode: Minus Front icon in the Pathfinder Panel.

9   Set the Fill to Black and the Stroke to [None].

10   Show all the hidden sublayers, and you are finished.

Complete

EXAMPLE 5: Line Pattern Fill

The following is an example of how to fill a shape with a line pattern. In this example, we will use a simple horizontal line pattern and the bezel outline as a clipping mask.

Actual Size

Enlarged

Blend of
repeating
lines

Clipping Mask

Start With the Text Face Bezel Example

To get started, you can continue from the previous Text Face Bezel example, or download the startup file (*EX05 Line Pattern Fill Start.ai*) from: *DavidTCurtis.wixsite.com/OrnamentalDesign*

Tip: If you cannot find the Layers panel, select *Window > Layers* in the menu or press *F7*.

If you see only two layers in the Layers Panel, click on the dropdown arrow next to the layer named, "Award Text".

Setup the Guides

Guide lines are import for making sure your line pattern will cover the entire area needed to fill a shape.

1   Start out by hiding all of the layers except the "Bezel Outline" and the "Guides" layer.

2   Select and unlock the "Guides" layer.

3   Select the top horizontal guide.

IMPORTANT! Before working with guides make sure the guides are not locked. Select: *View->Guides->Unlock Guides* from the top menu bar if you cannot select and move the guides.

4   Select *Object->Transform->Move* from the top menu.

5   In the Move Dialogue, input a Vertical Measurement of 11.25 mm.

6   Click on the Copy button.

Tip: The Move dialogue box is useful for making a copy of an item while moving it as well.

7   Click on the vertical ruler (y-axis) and drag to the left to create a vertical guide line. Position the guide on the left edge of the bezel outline.

8   Drag a second guide to the right edge of the bezel outline.

Create the Line Pattern (Blend)

Next, we will create the line pattern by drawing two lines and creating a Blend between them.

1   Lock the "Guides" layer.

2   Select and show the "Bezel Fill" sublayer.

3   Select the Line Segment Tool(▨).

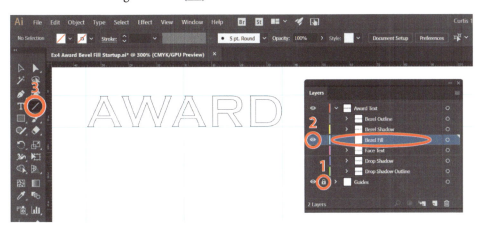

4   Click down on the top left corner of the guides, and drag across to the right corner. Hold down the Shift Key while doing this to make sure the line is perfectly horizontal. If you don't get the line straight or if it doesn't touch the guides, just select **Edit->Undo** and try again.

Tip: You can use the <Shift> key to constrain your lines to perfectly horizontal or vertical.

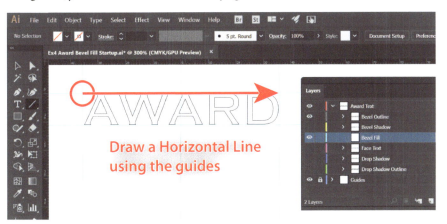

Draw a Horizontal Line using the guides

5   Set the Stroke Weight to 0.25pt.

6   Set the Stroke Color to Black.

7   Select **Object->Transform->Move** from the top menu.

8   In the Move Dialogue, input a Vertical Measurement of 11.25 mm.

9   Click on the Copy button.

10 Select everything in the "Bezel Fill" sublayer by clicking on the circle to the right of the sublayer name in the Layers Panel.

Select the top and bottom lines

11 Select *Object->Blend->Blend Options* from the top menu.

12 In the Blend Options dialog box, change the Spacing option from "Smooth Color" to "Specified Distance".

13 Set the Specified Distance to 0.3 mm.

14 Make sure the orientation is set to Align to Page.

15 Click on the OK button.

Tip: If you set the blend options before making the blend, those same blend options will be used for each subsequent blend you make.

16 Select *Object->Blend->Make Blend* from the top menu.

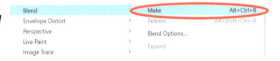

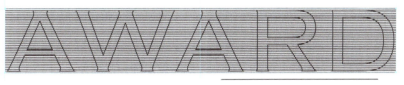

17 Select *Object->Blend->Expand*.

Note: Expanding a blend will convert the object into its individual elements.

Use the Bezel Outline as a Clipping Mask

Finally we will set the Bezel Outline as a clipping mask over the line pattern we just created.

1   Select everything in the "Bezel Outline" sublayer by clicking on the circle to the right of the sublayer name in the Layers Panel.

2   Select **Edit->Copy** from the top menu.

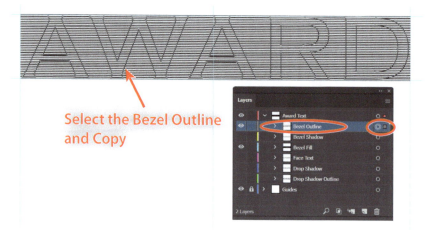

Select the Bezel Outline and Copy

3   Hide the "Bezel Outline" sublayer.

4   Select the "Bezel Fill" sublayer.

5   Select **Edit->Paste in Front** from the top menu.

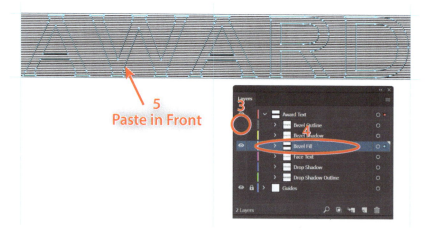

5
Paste in Front

6   Select everything in the "Bezel Fill" sublayer by clicking on the circle to the right of the sublayer name in the Layers Panel.

7   Select *Object->Clipping Mask->Make* from the top menu.

Note: A Clipping Mask is a shape that is used to "clip" the selected items that are behind the shape. It will appear as though the items are inside of the shape used as a clipping mask. Make sure the shape you want to be the Clipping Mask is in front of the other items.

8   Show all of the layers, and you are complete.

EXAMPLE 6: Crosshatch Pattern

The following is an example of how to create an object or text that is filled with a crosshatch pattern. In this example, we will replace the simple line pattern in the previous example with a more complex crosshatch pattern. The crosshatch will be made of two overlapping line patterns.

The first line pattern will be a blend of horizontal lines with a spacing of 0.5mm. The lines will vary in stroke weight, starting with 0.75pt and ending with 0.25pt.

The second line pattern will be a blend of diagonal lines with a spacing of 0.5mm. The lines will all have a stroke weight of 0.25pt and a 45-degree angle. You can experiment with different line widths, spacing and angles to get more interesting results.

Actual Size

Enlarged

Blend 1: Horizontal Lines
Spacing: 0.5mm
First Line Stroke Weight: 0.75pt
Last Line Stroke Weight: 0.25pt

Blend 2: Diagonal Lines (45-degrees)
Spacing: 0.5mm
Stroke Weight: 0.25pt

Crosshatch:
Blend 1 and Blend 2 Overlapped

To get started, you can continue from the previous Line Pattern Fill example, or download the startup file (*EX06 Crosshatch Pattern Start.ai*) from: *DavidTCurtis.wixsite.com/OrnamentalDesign*

Horizontal Line Blend 1
First we will create the horizontal line blend.

1   Hide all the sublayers except the "Bezel Fill" sublayer.

Tip: If you cannot find the Layers panel, select *Window > Layers* in the menu, or press *F7*.

2   Select everything in the "Bezel Fill" sublayer by clicking on the circle to the right of the sublayer name in the Layers Panel.

Select

3   Press the Delete Key or select *Edit->Clear* for the top menu bar.

Delete (Clear)

4   Select the Line Tool( ).

5   Set the Stroke Weight to 0.75pt.

6   Set the Stroke Color to Black.

7   Click on the top left corner of the rectangle indicated by the guides and drag
     a horizontal line to the top right corner. Hold down the Shift to make sure the
     line is perfectly horizontal.

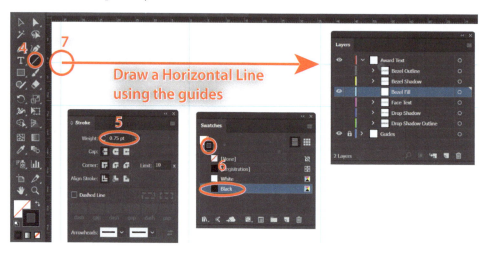

8   Select *Object->Transform->Move* from the top menu bar.

9   Set the Vertical to 11.25mm.

10   Click on the Copy button.

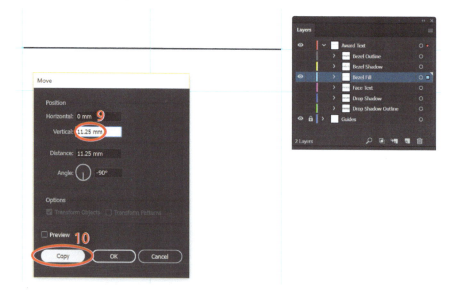

11   Set the Stroke Weight of the bottom line to 0.25pt.

Set Stroke Weight
to 0.25pt

12   Using the Selection Tool(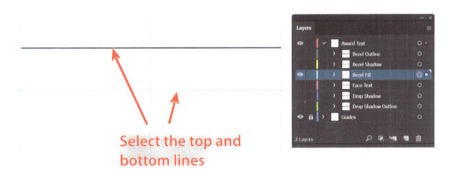), select both lines. You can do that by clicking on one line, then hold down the <Shift> key and selected the second line.

Select the top and
bottom lines

Tip: The items you select to make a Blend do not have to be identical. The Blend function will "morph" most of the attributes that change between the two items. However, not all attributes will work properly in a Blend. For example: if you use the Width Tool, you will need to perform an Expand Appearance before making a Blend.

13   Select *Object->Blend->Blend Options*.

14   Set the Spacing to "Specified Distance", enter 0.5mm and click the OK button.

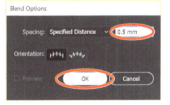

15   Select **Object->Blend->Make**.

Make Blend

16   Select **Object->Blend->Expand**.

Expand Blend

Diagonal Line Blend 2

Next, we will create the overlapping diagonal line blend.

1   Deselect the horizontal blend, by selecting Select->Deselect from the top menu bar. You can also just click somewhere in the empty space on the page.

2   Select the Line Tool( ).

3   Set the Stroke Weight to 0.25pt.

4   Set the Stroke Color to Black.

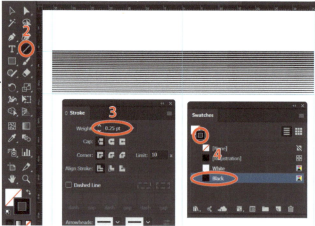

5   Hold down the <Shift> key while drawing a diagonal line that spans the entire height of the horizontal blend. The bottom right of the line should be on the bottom left corner of the horizontal blend. The top right of the line should be somewhere to the left along the top guide.

Hold Down the <Shift> Key

Tip: The <Shift> key will not only constrain your lines to perfectly horizontal or vertical, it will also constrain the Line Segment to a 45-degree angle also.

6   Find the Transform Panel.

7   Next, we need to calculate how far we need to copy and move this diagonal line to setup the second line in the blend. If you select both the diagonal line and the horizontal blend, the distance will be indicated in the width value on the transform panel. In the printing industry, the amount you wish to copy and move an object is called the "step".

8   Copy or write down the width value (step).

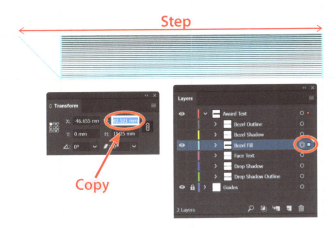

Step

Copy

9   Now, select only the diagonal line.

10   Select *Object->Transform->Move* from the top menu bar.

11   Set the Horizontal amount to the calculated width (step) you just copied, and set the Vertical amount to 0.

12   Select the Copy button.

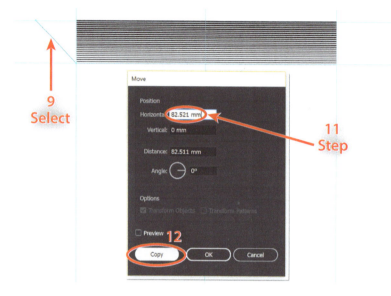

13   Select both diagonal lines, and check to make sure the Blend Options are still set to Specified Distance = 0.5mm

14   Select **Object->Blend->Make**.

Make Blend

15   Select **Object->Blend->Expand**.

Expand Blend

Bezel Outline Clipping Mask

Finally, we will apply a clipping mask to the crosshatch pattern. The clipping mask will be copied from the bezel outline.

1   Hide the "Bezel Fill" sublayer.

2   Show the "Bezel Outline" sublayer.

3   Select everything in the "Bezel Outline" sublayer by clicking on the circle to the right of the sublayer name in the Layers Panel.

4   Select **Edit->Copy** from the top menu bar.

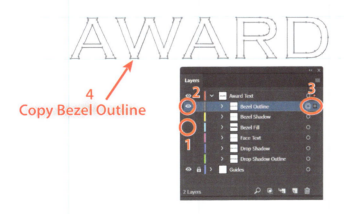

Copy Bezel Outline

5   Hide the "Bezel Outline" sublayer.

6   Show and Select the "Bezel Fill" sublayer.

7   Select *Edit->Paste in Front* from the top menu bar.

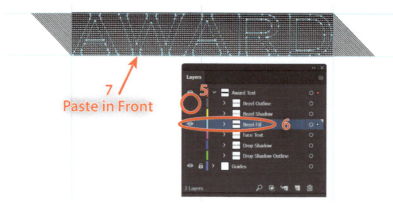

Note: Paste in Front is useful here since we need to make sure the bezel outline is the top-most item to be used as a Clipping Mask.

8   Select everything in the "Bezel Fill" sublayer by clicking on the circle to the right of the sublayer name in the Layers Panel.

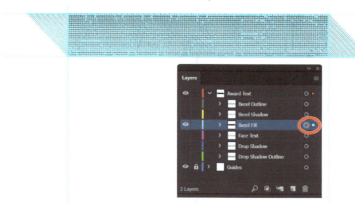

9   Select *Object->Clipping Mask->Make* from the top menu bar.

10   Show all of the layers, and you are complete.

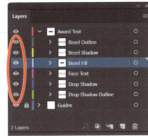

EXAMPLE 7: Banner Text (Warp Method)

The following is an example of how to create banner text using the Warp Effect. The Warp Effect is a quick, convenient solution, but can be problematic when applied to a complex, multi-layered design. Using the Warp Effect on a complex multi-layer design can cause the layers to get out of alignment. This is due to how the Warp Effect calculates the bounding box of separate layers and objects. If you are using a clipping mask, which clips a large embedded object, like we did in the crosshatch example, the Warp Effect may have unpredictable results.

In this example, we will apply the Warp Effect in two ways. First, we will use the Warp Effect on our previous example "Award" text after the bezel / drop shadow methods have been applied. Second, we will use the Warp Effect on the "Award" text before the bezel / drop shadow methods are applied. You can see the subtle differences below.

Warp Effect Applied After Bezel / Drop Shadow

Warp Effect Applied Before Bezel / Drop Shadow

To get started, you can continue from the previous Line Pattern Fill example, or download the startup file (*EX07 Warp Banner Text Part 1 Start.ai*) from: *DavidTCurtis.wixsite.com/OrnamentalDesign*

Tip: If you cannot find the Layers panel, select *Window > Layers* in the menu or press *F7*.

If you see only two layers in the Layers Panel, click on the dropdown arrow next to the layer named, "Award Text".

Warp Effect Applied After Bezel / Drop Shadow

First, we will apply the Warp Effect to the "Award" text that already has a bezel and drop shadow.

1   Start with the "AWARD" text complete with Contoured Drop Shadow and Line Pattern Bezel Fill

2   Select the "Award Text" top layer.

3   Select everything in the "Award Text" top layer by clicking on the small circle to the right of the layer name in the Layers Panel. Important: Make sure you select everything using the small circle in the Layers Panel, otherwise the Warp Effect will get the separate sublayers out of alignment.

4   Select **Effect->Warp->Arc...** from the top menu bar.

5   In the Warp dialogue box, set the Style to "Arc" and use the Horizontal option.

6   Set the Bend amount to 20%.

7   Select OK.

Note: There are many "Styles" of Warp that can be applied. If you want to see what they look like, click the Preview Checkbox and experiment with the different Warp Styles.

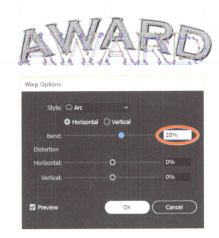

8   Select **Object->Expand Appearance**.

Warp Effect Applied Before Bezel / Drop Shadow

Next, we will apply the Warp Effect to the plain text before adding a drop shadow and bezel. This will be a brief review of the contoured drop shadow and filled bezel methods from previous examples.

1   If there is any Award text artwork present on the page, clear (delete) it. Make sure you just have the guides and empty sublayers in setup as follows:

> **Layers**
> > Award Text
> > > Bezel Outline
> > > Bezel Shadow
> > > Bezel Fill
> > > Face Text
> > > Drop Shadow
> > > Drop Shadow Outline
> > Guides

2   Select the "Face Text" sublayer.

3   Select the Type Tool (⊞).

4   Click somewhere near the guides. (We will move the text to the correct position later).

5   Set the Font to "Copperplate Gothic Bold", 48pt.

6   Type "AWARD" in all caps.

7   Click on the Selection Tool (▷) .

8   Select **Effect->Warp->Arc...** from the top menu bar.

9   In the Warp dialogue box, set the Style to "Arc" and use the Horizontal option.

10   Set the Bend amount to 20%.

11   Select OK.

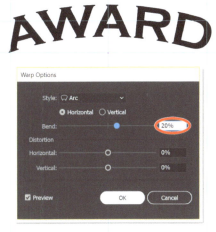

12 Select **Object->Expand Appearance** from the top menu bar.

All of the following steps are a review of the contoured drop shadow and bezel methods in the previous examples.

13 Set the Stroke Weight to 0.25pt.

14 Set the Fill color to White and the Stroke Color to Black.

15 Set the origin to the intersection of the top center guides. (If not done already)

16 Make sure the "AWARD" text is selected and use the Transform Panel to move the "AWARD" text to (0,0)
.

Transform Panel		
Reference Point: **Top Center**	X: *0 mm* Y: *0 mm* Rotate: *0°*	W: *71.462 mm* H: *11.286 mm* Shear: *0°*

17 Copy the "AWARD" text.

16

17
Copy

18   Hide the "Face Text" sublayer.

19   Select the "Drop Shadow" sublayer.

20   Select **Edit->Paste in Place** from the top menu.

21   Use the Transform Panel to move the drop shadow down 0.5 mm and to the right 0.5 mm.

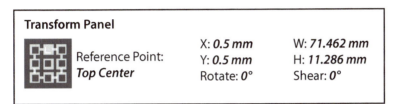

Transform Panel

Reference Point: **Top Center**

X: *0.5 mm*   W: *71.462 mm*
Y: *0.5 mm*   H: *11.286 mm*
Rotate: *0°*   Shear: *0°*

22   Set the drop shadow fill to Black, and set the drop shadow stroke to White.

23   Set the Stroke Weight to 0.25pt, and set Align Stroke to Inside.

24   Copy the Drop Shadow artwork.

25   Hide the "Drop Shadow" sublayer.

26   Select the "Drop Shadow Outline" sublayer.

27   Select **Edit->Paste in Place** from the top menu.

28   Set the Fill to White, and set the Stroke Color to Black.

29   Set the Stroke Weight to 0.25pt, and set the Align Stroke to Outside.

Tip: As you complete the artwork for each sublayer, it's a good idea to show/hide the other layers to make sure the artwork stays aligned and you are getting the results you want.

30   Hide the "Drop Shadow Outline" sublayer.

31   Show the "Face Text" sublayer.

32   Select the Face Text.

33   Select **Object->Path->Offset Path...** from the top menu bar.

34 Set the Offset Path settings to:
 Offset: -0.3mm
 Joins: Miter (Default)
 Miter Limit: 4 (Default)
Select the OK Button.

IMPORTANT!
Make sure you do the cut right after the offset path is completed, because only the newly generated artwork will be selected at that time. If you deselect, the new offset path will be grouped with the original artwork. Then, you would have to ungroup and select each piece of the new artwork individually.

35 Select **Edit->Cut** from the top menu bar.

36 Hide the "Face Text" sublayer.

37 Show and select the "Bezel Outline" sublayer.

38 Select **Edit->Paste in Place** from the top menu.

39 Select **Object->Compound Path->Make**.

40 Set the Fill to [None].

IMPORTANT!
Make sure you perform the "Compound Path" function, or the next steps involving the Pathfinder will not work. Making a compound path causes the program to treat all the pieces as one object rather than as separate elements.

Paste in Place

41 Copy the Bezel Outline.

42 Hide the "Bezel Outline" sublayer.

43 Select the "Bezel Shadow" sublayer.

44 Select **Edit->Paste in Place** from the top menu.

Paste in Place

45 Select *Object->Transform->Move* from the top menu.

In the Move Dialogue, input the following:
Distance: 0.2mm
Angle: -45
Then select the Copy button.

46 Select everything in the "Bezel Shadow" sublayer.

47 Click on the Shape Mode: Minus Front icon in the Pathfinder Panel.

48 Set the Fill Color to Black, and set the Stroke Color to [None].

49 Hide the "Bezel Drop Shadow" sublayer, and show the "Bezel Outline" layer.

50 Select and unlock the "Guides" layer.

51 Move the guides to a position just outside of the Bezel Outline artwork.

52 Lock the "Guides" layer.

53 Hide the "Bezel Outline" sublayer.

54   Show and select the "Bezel Fill" sublayer.

55   Select the Line Segment Tool(▱).

56   Set the Stroke Weight to 0.25pt.

57   Set the Stroke Color to Black.

58   Draw two lines at the top and bottom of the rectangle formed by the guides.

59   Select both lines.

60   Select **Object->Blend->Blend Options...** from the top menu bar.

61   In the Blend Options dialog box,
setup the following:
Spacing: **Specified Distance**
Distance: **0.3 mm**

Click on the OK button.

62   Select **Object->Blend->Make** from
the top menu bar.

63 Show the "Bezel Outline" sublayer.

64 Select and Copy the Bezel Outline.

65 Hide the "Bezel Outline" sublayer.

66 Select the "Bezel Fill" sublayer.

67 Select **Edit->Paste in Front** from the top menu bar.

68 Select everything in the "Bezel Fill" sublayer.

69 Select **Object->Clipping Mask->Make** from the top menu bar.

Copy Bezel Outline and
Make Clipping Mask

70 Show all layers and you are complete.

EXAMPLE 8: Banner Text (Path Method)

The following is an example of how to create banner text using the Type on a Path tool. This method is more effective than the warp method if the banner text needs to follow a complex path, or fit within an existing piece of artwork.

In this example, we will create a piece of artwork that looks like a typical "Swallowtail" banner, and then type some text that fits within the banner artwork.

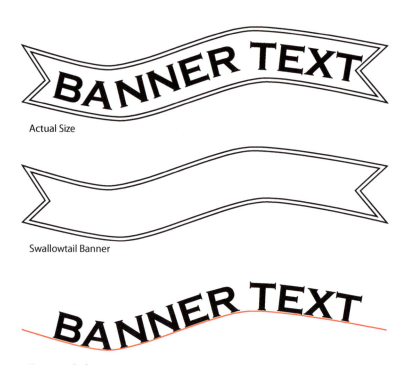

Actual Size

Swallowtail Banner

Type on a Path

To get started, you can create a new file from scratch, or download the startup file (*EX08 Banner Text Path Method Start.ai*) from:
DavidTCurtis.wixsite.com/OrnamentalDesign

File Setup

First, we will setup a new document with a page custom sized for the artwork.

1   Select **File->New...** from the top menu bar.

2   In the New Document Dialogue use the following settings:
Name: **Banner Text**
Number of Artboards: **1**
Size: **Custom**
Units: **Millimeters**
Width: **100 mm**
Height: **35 mm**
Orientation: **Landscape** (Horizontal)
Bleed: **0 mm** (for all four options: Top, Bottom...)
Color Mode: **CMYK**
Raster Effects: **High (300ppi)**
Preview Mode: **Default**

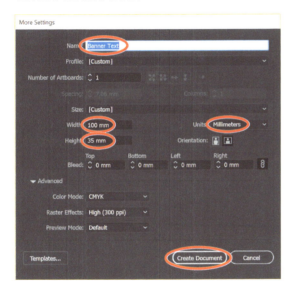

3   Select **View->Fit Artboard in Window** from the top menu bar.

Swallowtail Banner Artwork

Next, we will create a simple swallowtail banner.

1   In the Layers panel, change the name of "Layer 1" to "Guides".
(Double-click on the layer name to change the text.)

2   Select **View->Rulers->Show Rulers** from the top menu bar.

3   Click down on the top ruler, and drag down a guide.
     Use the Transform panel to position the guide as follows:

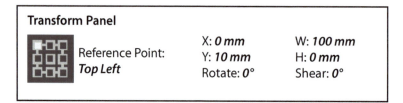

Transform Panel

Reference Point: **Top Left**

X: *0 mm*	W: *100 mm*
Y: *10 mm*	H: *0 mm*
Rotate: *0°*	Shear: *0°*

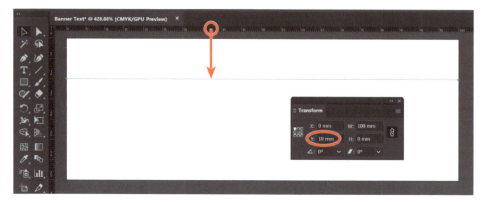

4   Drag another guide from the top ruler, and position it as follows:

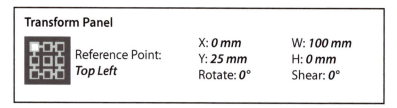

Transform Panel

Reference Point: **Top Left**

X: *0 mm*	W: *100 mm*
Y: *25 mm*	H: *0 mm*
Rotate: *0°*	Shear: *0°*

5   Click down on the left ruler, and drag across a guide.
Use the Transform panel to position the guide as follows:

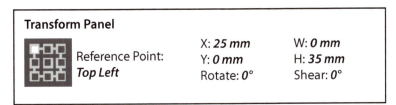

Transform Panel

Reference Point: **Top Left**

X: *25 mm*   W: *0 mm*
Y: *0 mm*   H: *35 mm*
Rotate: *0°*   Shear: *0°*

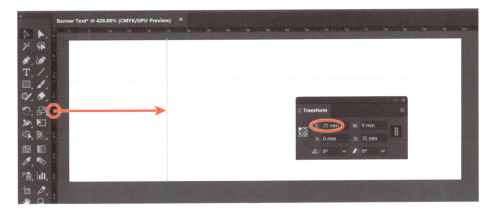

6   Drag another guide from the left ruler, and position it as follows:

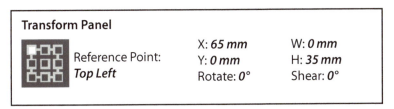

Transform Panel

Reference Point: **Top Left**

X: *65 mm*   W: *0 mm*
Y: *0 mm*   H: *35 mm*
Rotate: *0°*   Shear: *0°*

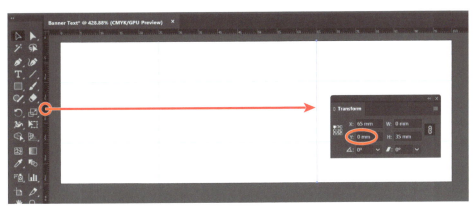

7   Lock the "Guides" layer.

8   Create a new layer.

9   Name the new layer "Banner".

10   Select the Rectangle Tool (▣).

11   Set the Stroke Color to Black

12   Set the Stroke Weight to 1pt.

13   Draw a rectangle between the top and bottom guides that spans the entire with of the page.

14   Although it is not critical for this example, you can use the Transform Panel to set the exact size and position of the rectangle as follows:

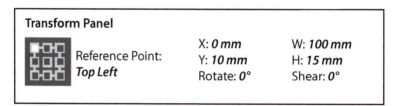

15   Select the Add Anchor Point Tool (▨). You can find it by clicking and holding down on the Pen Tool(▨).

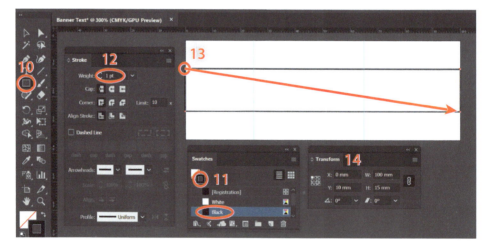

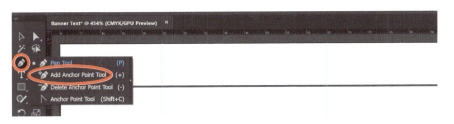

Tip: You Add Anchor Points by clicking on the line where you want to add the points.

16   Add anchor points where the vertical guides intersect the rectangle.

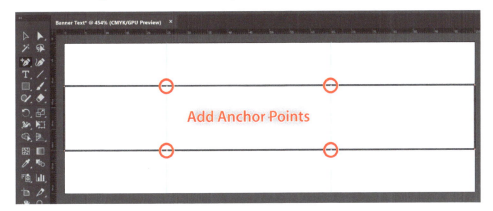

Add Anchor Points

Note: The main difference between the Selection Tool and the Direct Selection Tool, is that the Selection Tool will select an entire object made up of many Anchor Points, but the Direct Selection Tool will select individual Anchor Points within an object.

17   Click on the Direct Selection Tool ([▶]).

18   Select all of the new anchor points you just added to the rectangle.

IMPORTANT: Make Sure You Use the Direct Selection Tool

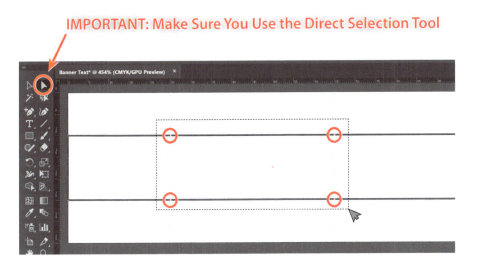

19 Select **Object->Transform->Rotate...** from the top menu bar.

20 In the Rotate dialogue box, set the angle to 15 degrees, then click the OK button.

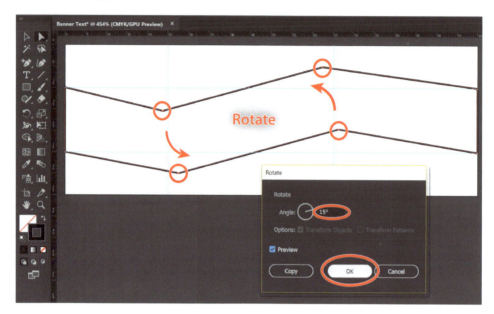

21 While the anchor points are still selected, click on the "Convert selected anchor points to smooth" button (□). (*Yes, that is the actual name of the button*)

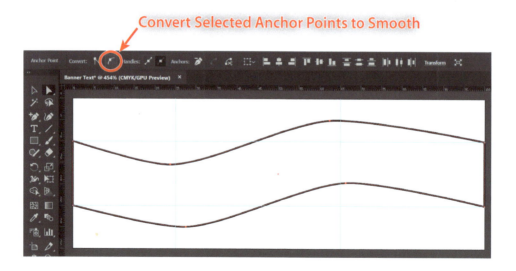

22   Select the Add Anchor Point Tool ( ).

23   Add anchor points to the middle of the vertical lines in the banner.

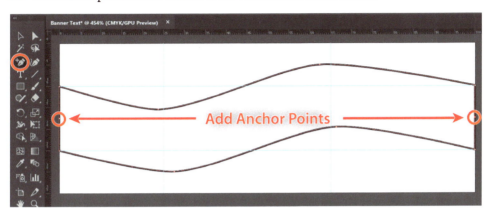

24   Click on the Direct Selection Tool ( ).

25   Drag the new anchor points towards the center of the banner to create a "Swallow Tail" look to the banner.

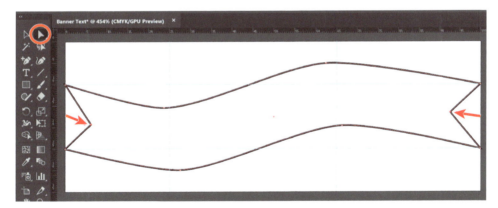

Banner Text
Next, we will create banner text that will fit perfectly inside of the banner artwork.

1   In the Layers panel submenu, select Duplicate "Banner".

2   Hide the "Banner" layer.

3   Change the "Banner copy" layer name to "Banner Text".

4   Using the Direct Selection Tool (▶), select all of the anchor points below the top line of the banner.

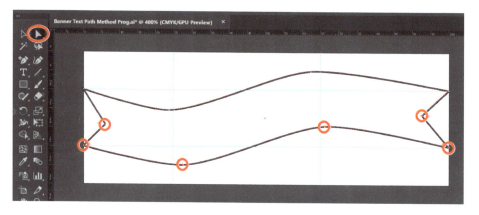

5   Select **Edit->Clear** from the top menu bar, or press the <Delete> key to delete the selected anchor points.

6   Click on the Selection Tool (▶).|

7   Move the banner line segment down to just below the middle of the guides. You can use the arrow keys or drag it downward.

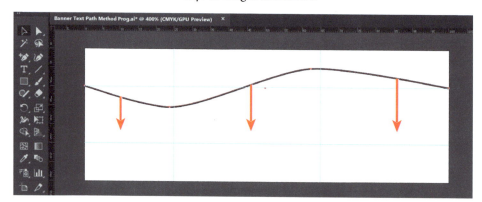

8   Select the Type on a Path Tool (⬦). You can find it by clicking and holding down on the Type Tool (T).|

9   In the Paragraph Panel, select the Align Center button.

10   In the Character Panel, select the "Copperplate Gothic Bold" font and set the font size to 30pt.

11   Click on the anchor point on the left side of the page.

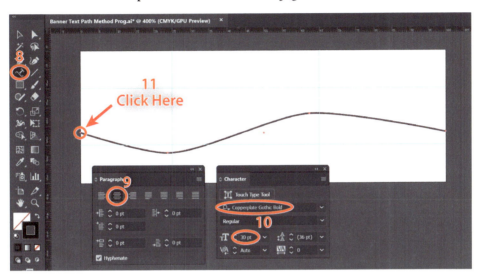

12   Type "BANNER TEXT" in all caps.

13 Show the "Banner" Layer.

14 Click on the Selection Tool ( ).

15 Reposition the banner text to fit in the center of the banner artwork.

Tip: You can use the arrow-keys to make small adjustments to the position of a selected item.

16 Select the banner artwork.

17 Select **Object->Path->Offset Path…** from the top menu bar.

18 In the Offset Path dialogue box set the Offset to **-1 mm** and click OK.

19 You should now be complete.

Complete

The Golden Ratio

The "Golden Ratio" is a math ratio often used by artists and designers to make a decision regarding how much larger or smaller to make shapes and curves in relation to one another in a piece of artwork. The concept of the golden ratio has been around since before the ancient times of Greek Architecture, and is still used today to decide the proportions for cell phones and television screens. One of the simplest ways to describe the golden ratio is with the Fibonacci sequence.

The **Fibonacci Sequence** is a series of numbers, where each number is equal to the sum of the two preceding numbers.

$$a + b = c \qquad 1 + 2 = 3$$
$$b + c = d \qquad 2 + 3 = 5$$
$$c + d = e \qquad 3 + 5 = 8$$
$$d + e = f \qquad 5 + 8 = 13$$

Therefore, the Fibonacci sequence is:

0, 1, 1, 2, 3, 5, 8, 13, 21...

Mathematicians have calculated the golden ratio to be 1:1.618. That means if you want to create two shapes that follow the golden ratio, you would multiply the size by 1.618 to make a larger shape, or divide by 1.618 to make a smaller shape. This holds true for the Fibonacci sequence if you round off the numbers to integers.

Use the Fibonacci sequence to decide the next size up or down.

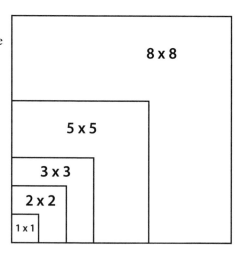

The Golden Rectangle

To create a golden rectangle, start with one side equal to a number in the Fibonacci sequence, and then the adjacent side should have a length equal to the next number in the sequence.

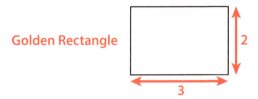

Next, add a square to the longer of the two sides. Notice, that the resulting rectangle will also be a golden rectangle.

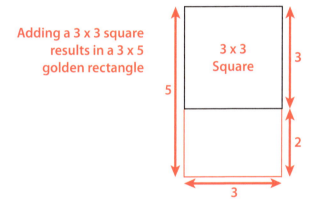

Keep repeating the process, and you will always end up with a golden rectangle with side lengths that follow the Fibonacci sequence.

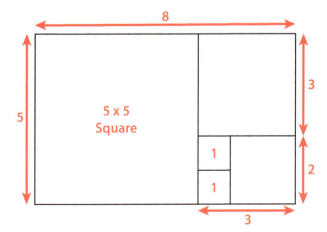

The Golden Spiral

We can use the same process to create a golden spiral.

Start with a 5 x 8 rectangle and create a 5 x 5 square on the inside. Draw an arc through the 5 x 5 square as shown here.

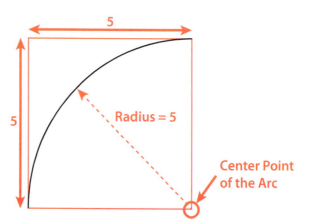

Now, make an adjacent 3 x 3 square, and draw another arc.

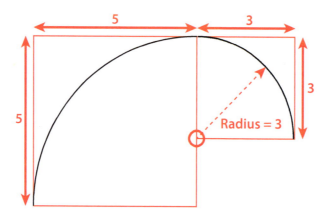

Continue with adjacent 2 x 2 and 1 x 1 squares to complete the spiral.

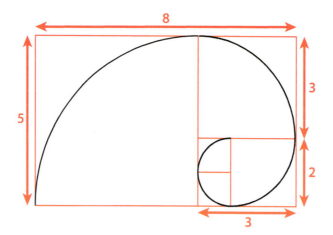

You can create an infinite number of combinations of spirals. If you use the Fibonacci sequence to determine your size and spacing, you can be sure that your artwork will have a look of balance and beauty. Throughout this chapter, you will use the golden ratio and Fibonacci sequence to create several ornamental designs.

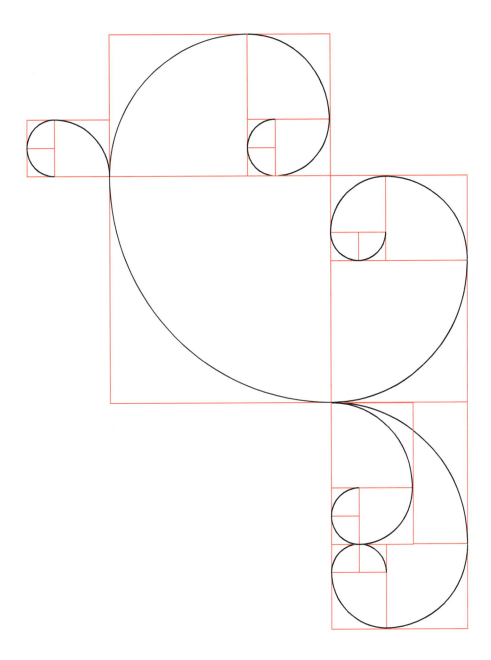

How to Use the Spiral Tool in ADOBE® ILLUSTRATOR® CC

Adobe Illustrator has a built-in Spiral Tool that can be a bit confusing if you do not understand how it works. The tool's interface is based on you using the pointer (mouse) to draw the initial arc of the spiral. The point where you first click will be the center point of the arc, and the distance you drag the pointer will be the radius of the initial arc of the spiral.

You can find the Spiral Tool (⊙) by clicking and holding down on the Line Segment Tool(⁄).

Click anywhere on the page to show the Spiral Dialogue Box.

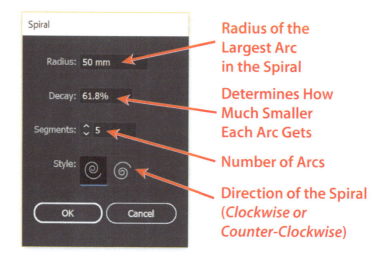

Radius of the Largest Arc in the Spiral

Determines How Much Smaller Each Arc Gets

Number of Arcs

Direction of the Spiral (*Clockwise or Counter-Clockwise*)

What happens when you change the decay percentage in a spiral?

Decay:

50%

60%

70%

80%

90%

The Spiral Dialogue Box has the following inputs:

Radius: This is the radius of the largest or initial arc in the spiral.

Decay: The decay value determines what percentage the radius is reduced in each arc of the spiral. To create a golden spiral, use 61.8%, which is equivalent to the golden ratio 1:1.618. This means that if you enter 50mm in the Radius value, then the spiral will be drawn with an initial arc with a 50mm radius. The next arc will have a 30mm radius, and then 20mm and so on...

Segments: The number of segments is equal to the number of arcs in the spiral.

Style: The Style determines whether the spiral rotates clockwise or counter-clockwise.

Whenever you use the Spiral tool, I recommend drawing a square as a guide for the initial arc of the spiral like shown below.

Clicking down on the mouse sets the center point of the initial arc in the spiral.

Drag outward from the center point to set the radius.

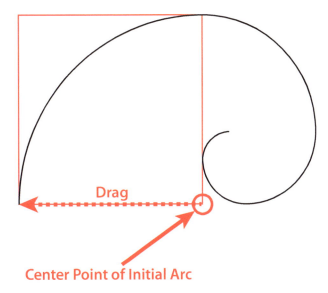

If you just click without dragging the pointer, a spiral will be drawn using an initial arc with a radius equal to the radius specified in the Spiral Dialogue Box.

EXAMPLE 9: C-Shape Spiral

The following is an example of how to create a spiral design in the shape of the letter "C". This method is basically just two golden spirals joined together. We will use the Width Tool to create a shape from the spiral lines, and then offset the path to add detail.

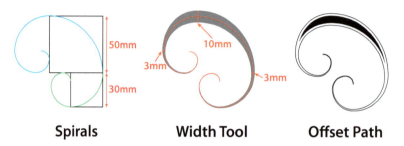

Spirals   **Width Tool**   **Offset Path**

File Setup

First, we will setup a new document with a page custom sized for the artwork.

1   Select *File->New...* from the top menu bar.

2   In the New Document Dialogue use the following settings:

Name: **C-Shape Spiral**
Number of Artboards: **1**

Size: **Custom**
Units: **Millimeters**
Width: **240 mm**
Height: **120 mm**
Orientation: **Landscape** (Horizontal)

Bleed: **0 mm** (for all four options: Top, Bottom…)

Color Mode: **CMYK**
Raster Effects: **High (300ppi)**
Preview Mode: **Default**

3   Select *View->Fit Artboard* in Window from the top menu bar.

4   Select *View->Rulers->Show Rulers* from the top menu bar.

5   Select *Edit->Preferences->Guides & Grid...*

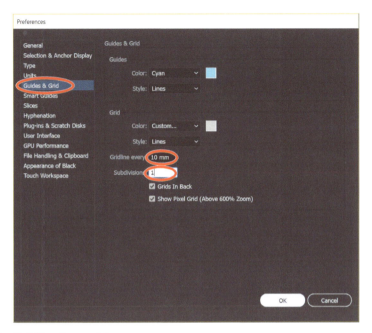

6   Set Gridline Every: **10mm**.

7   Set Subdivisions: **1**.

8   Select *View->Show Grid*.

9   Select *View->Snap to Grid*.

10   Rename "Layer 1" as "Guides".

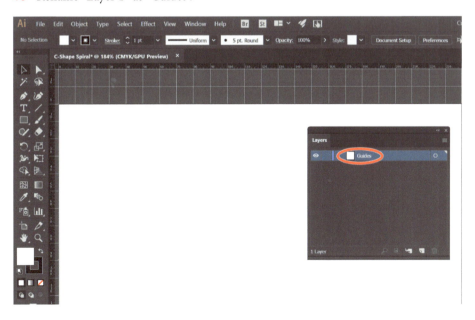

11 Drag a vertical guide out to 120mm. (This will be the center line)

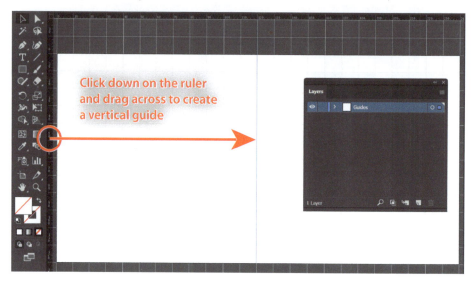

Spiral Guides
Next, we will create two boxes to use as guides for creating the spirals.

1 Select the Rectangle Tool (▣).

2 Set the Stroke Weight to 1pt.

3 Set the Stroke Color to Black and the Fill to [None].

4 Draw a 50x50mm square that is 20mm from the top and on the left side of the center line.

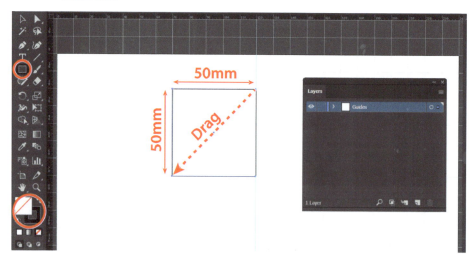

5   Draw a 30x30mm square that is directly below the previous square and on left side of the center line.

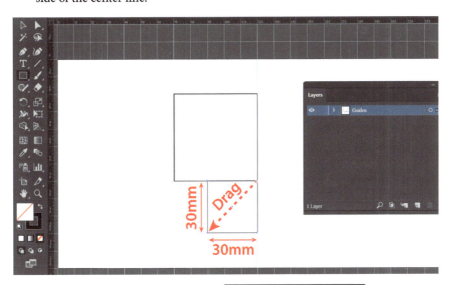

6   Lock the "Guides" layer.

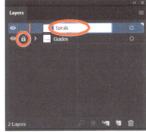

Spirals

Next, we will create two spirals.

1   Create a new layer named "Spirals".

2   Select the Spiral Tool ().

3   Make sure the stroke weight is 1pt, the stroke color is Black and the fill is set to [None].

Tip: You can find the Spiral Tool (⊚) by clicking and holding down on the Line Segment Tool(╱).

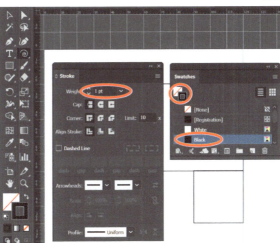

4   Click on the bottom left corner of the 50x50mm square.

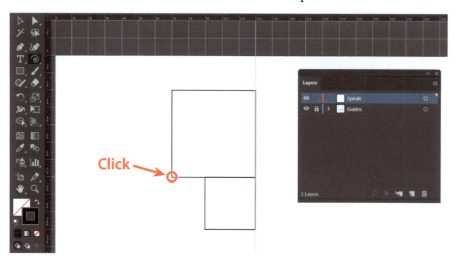

What happens if you change the number of segments in a spiral?

Number of Segments:

3

4

5

6

5   In the Spiral dialogue, set the following:
    Radius: **50mm**
    Decay: **61.8%**
    Segments: **5**
    Style: **Counter-clockwise**

6   Click on the top left of the 30x30 square.

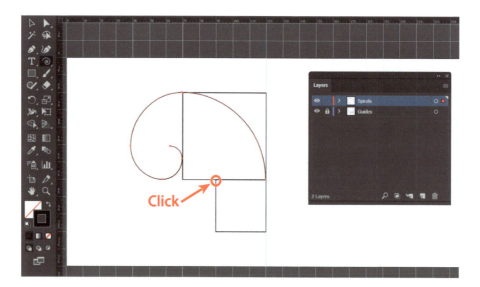

7   In the Spiral dialogue, set the following:
    Radius: **30mm**
    Decay: **61.8%**
    Segments: **4**
    Style: **Clockwise**

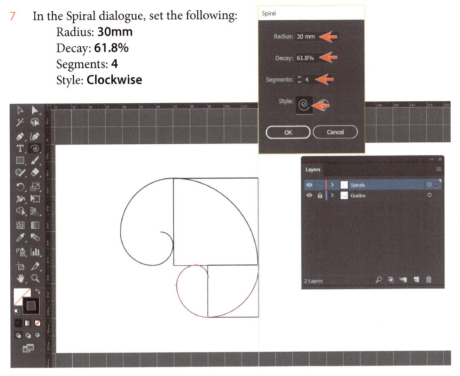

Note: If you want the spirals on both sides of the C-shape to match, just make sure the smaller spiral has one less segment than the larger spiral.

Connecting the Spirals
Next, we will connect the two spirals into one path.

1   Hide the "Guides" layer.

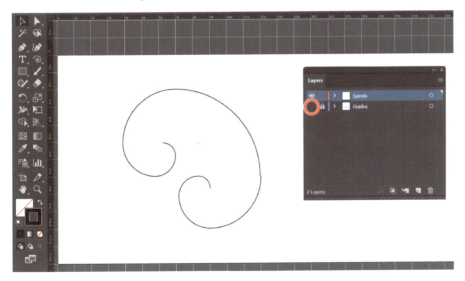

2   Select the Zoom Tool (🔍) and zoom in very close to where the two spirals should connect.

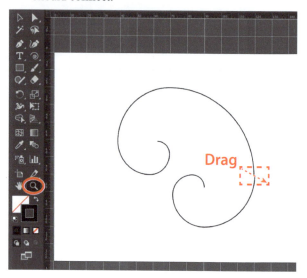

3   Click on the Selection Tool (▶), and move the top spiral so that the end of the path lines up perfectly with the grid.

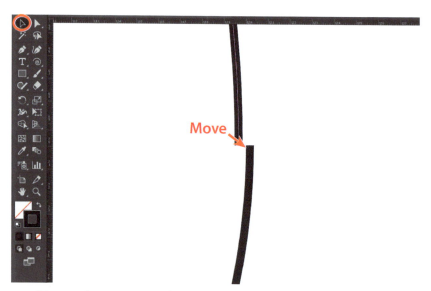

(You may have to move it far away and then back again to get it lined up perfectly.)

4   Now move the bottom spiral so that the end of the path lines up perfectly with the top spiral.

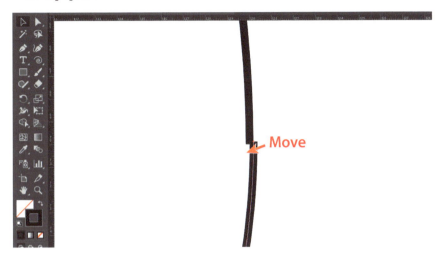

Tip: If you are having difficulty getting the end points perfectly aligned, you can try using the Align Panel. You can find the Align Panel by selecting *Window->Align* in the top menu bar.

Use the Direct Selection Tool (), and select the end points. Then, click on the Horizontal Align Center button and the Vertical Align Center button.

5   Click on the Direct Selection Tool (), and select the end points of both spirals.

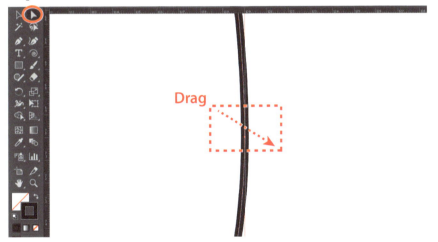

6   Select *Object->Path->Join* from the top menu bar.

7   Select *View->Fit All in Window*, and you should see that both spirals are now one path.

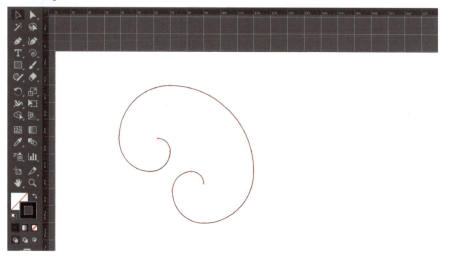

Use the Width Tool to Make an Interesting Spiral Design
Next, we will use the Width Tool to create a spiral shape that has volume.

1   Select the Line Width Tool (![icon]).

2   Select *View->Snap to Grid* to turn off the Snap to Grid function.

3   Click and drag vertically on the top most point of the spiral until the width is approximately 10mm.

Tip: If the little box showing the line width does not show up, then you probably need to turn off Snap to Grid.

Make sure there is not a checkmark on the menu item:
View->Snap to Grid

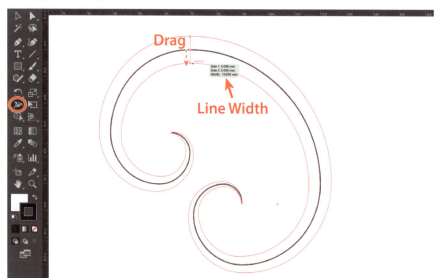

4   Click and drag horizontally on the left most point of the spiral until the width is approximately 3mm.

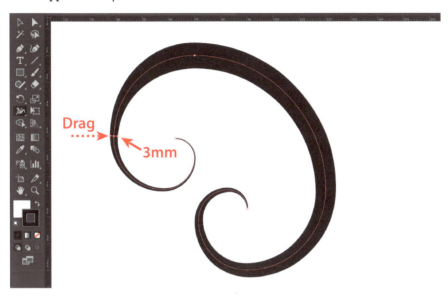

5   Click and drag horizontally on the right most point of the spiral until the width is approximately 3mm.

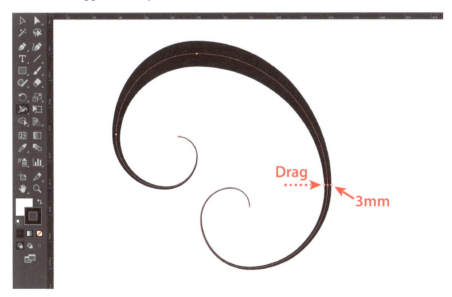

6   Click on the Selection Tool (▶), and select the spiral shape.

7   Select *Object->Path->Outline Stroke* from the top menu bar.

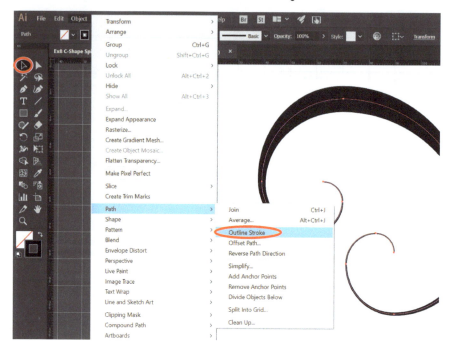

8   Set the fill color to White, the Stroke color to Black and the Stroke Weight to 1pt.

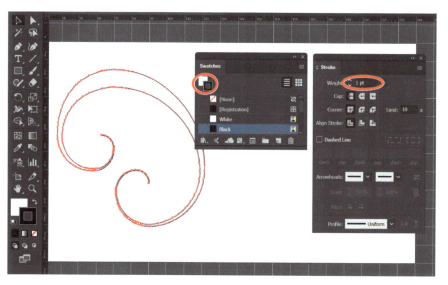

9   Select **Object->Path->Offset Path…** from the top menu bar.

10   In the Offset Path dialogue, set the following:
         Offset: **-2mm**
         Joins: **Miter**
         Miter Limit: **4**

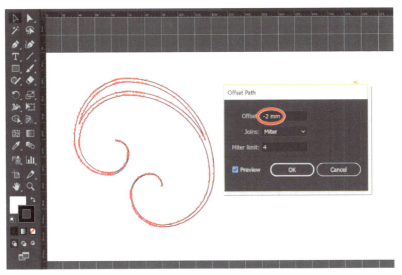

11   Select the crescent shape, and set the Fill Color to Black and the Stroke Color to [None]

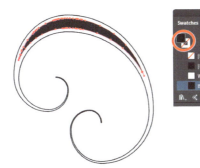

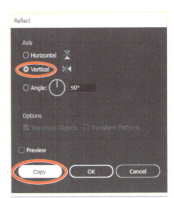

You can use **Object->Transform->Reflect** to create a mirror image and duplicate.

EXAMPLE 10: S-Shape Spiral

The following is an example of how to create a spiral design in the shape of the letter "S". This method is basically just two golden spirals joined together. We will use the Width Tool to create a shape from the spiral lines, and then offset the path to add detail.

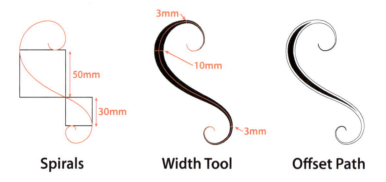

Spirals   **Width Tool**   **Offset Path**

File Setup

First, we will setup a new document with a page custom sized for the artwork.

1   Select *File->New...* from the top menu bar.

2   In the New Document Dialogue use the following settings:

Name: **S-Shape Spiral**
Number of Artboards: **1**
Size: **Custom**
Units: **Millimeters**
Width: **180 mm**
Height: **150 mm**
Orientation: **Landscape** (Horizontal)

Bleed: **0 mm** (for all four options: Top, Bottom...)

Color Mode: **CMYK**
Raster Effects: **High (300ppi)**
Preview Mode: **Default**

3   Select *View->Fit Artboard in Window* from the top menu bar.

4   Select *View->Rulers->Show Rulers* from the top menu bar.

5   Select *Edit->Preferences->Guides & Grid...* from the top menu bar.

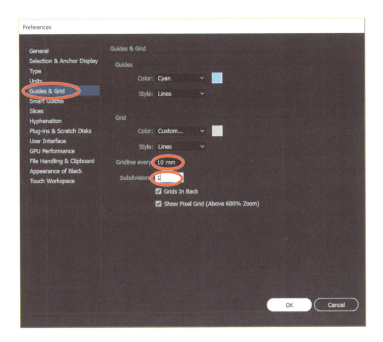

6   Set Gridline Every: **10mm**.

7   Set Subdivisions: **1**.

8   Select **View->Show Grid** from the top menu bar..

9   Select **View->Snap to Grid** from the top menu bar..

10   Rename "Layer 1" as "Guides"

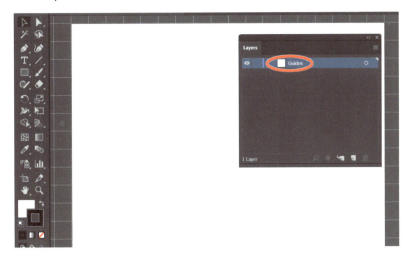

Spiral Guides

Next, we will create two boxes to use as guides for creating the spirals

1   Select the Rectangle Tool (▢).

2   Set the Stroke Weight to 1pt.

3   Set the Stroke Color to Black and the Fill to [None].

4   Draw a 50x50mm square that is 40mm from the top and 10mm from the left.

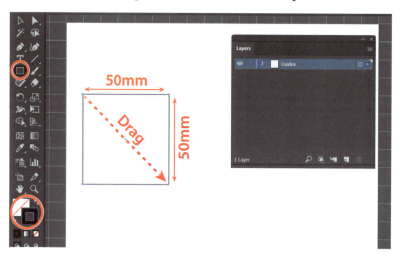

5   Draw a 30x30mm square that is positioned below and to the right of the previous square.

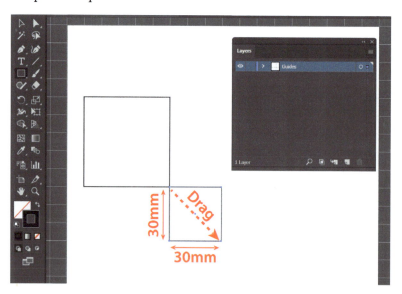

6   Lock the "Guides" layer.

Spirals
Next, we will create two spirals.

1   Create a new layer named "Spirals".

2   Select the Spiral Tool (⊚).

3   Make sure the stroke weight is 1pt, the stroke color is Black and the fill is set to [None].

Tip: You can find the Spiral Tool (⊚) by clicking and holding down on the Line Segment Tool(╱).

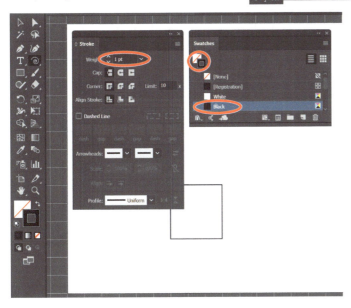

4   Click anywhere on the page.

5   In the Spiral dialogue, set the following:
Radius: **50mm**
Decay: **61.8%**
Segments: **5**
Style: **Clockwise**

6   Select **Edit-Clear** to delete the spiral you just made. (We just needed to setup the Spiral Dialogue Box with the correct values.)

7   Click on the top right corner of the 50x50mm box and drag down to the bottom right corner.

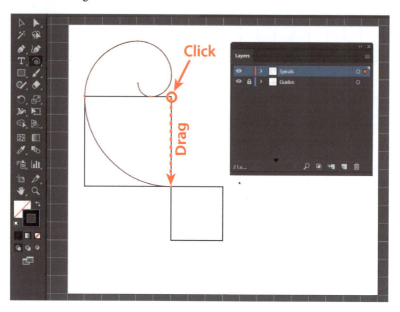

8   Click on the bottom left corner of the 30x30mm box and drag up to the top left corner.

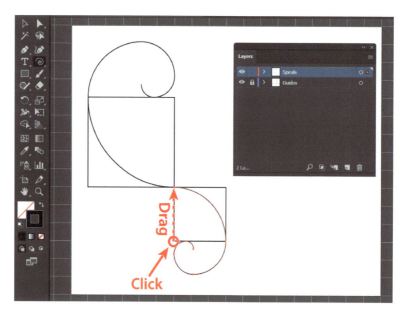

Connecting the Spirals

Next, we will connect the two spirals into one path.

1   Hide the "Guides" layer.

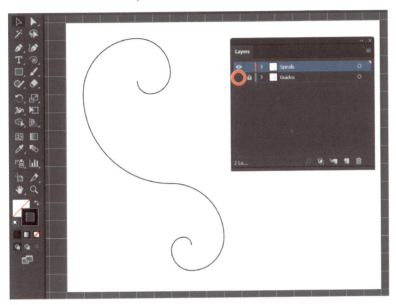

2   Select the Zoom Tool (🔍), and zoom in very close to where the two spirals should connect.

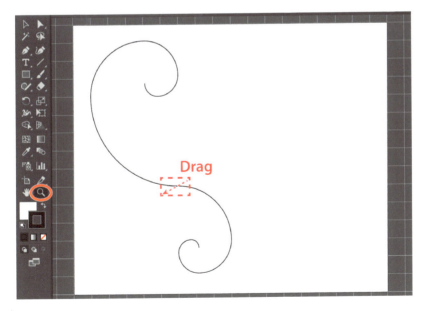

3   Click on the Selection Tool (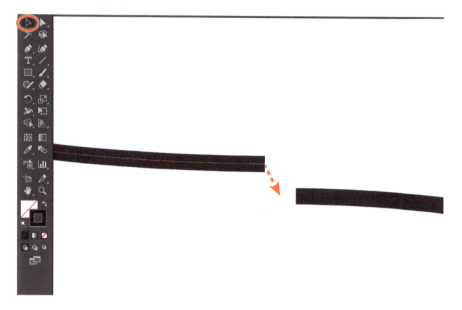), and move the top spiral so that the end of the path lines up perfectly with the grid. (You may have to move it far away and then back again.)

Tip: If you are having difficulty getting the end points perfectly aligned, you can try using the Align Panel. You can find the Align Panel by selecting *Window->Align* in the top menu bar.

Use the Direct Selection Tool (), and select the end points. Then, click on the Horizontal Align Center button and the Vertical Align Center button.

4   Now move the bottom spiral so that the end of the path lines up perfectly with the top spiral.

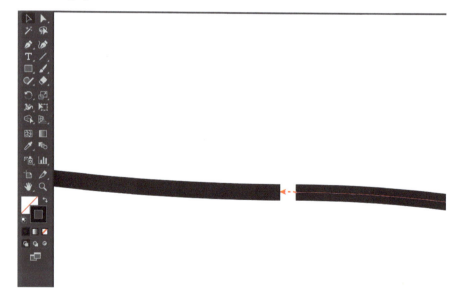

5   Click on the Direct Selection Tool (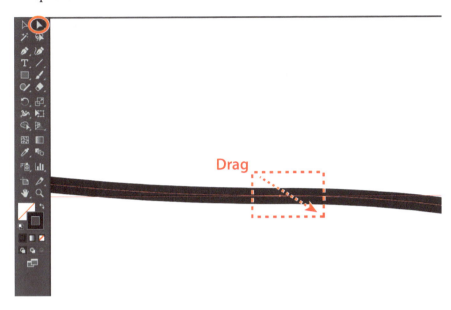), and select the end points of both spirals.

Drag

6   Select *Object->Path->Join* from the top menu bar.

7   Select *View->Fit All in Window*, and you should see that both spirals are now one path.

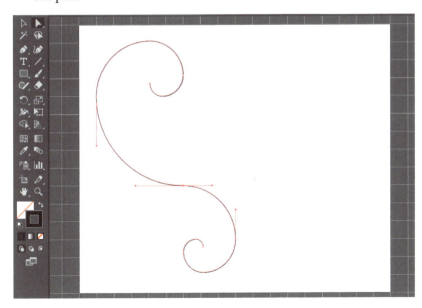

Note: In order for the curve between the two spirals to look natural, it is critical that the two end points join together as one anchor point. To join two end points so that they become one anchor point, they must be perfectly overlapping. If the two end points are not perfectly aligned, the Join function will add a line segment to bridge the gap between the two end points.

8 Click on the Convert Selected Anchor Points to Corner button. (If nothing happens, try clicking on the Convert Selected Anchor Points to Smooth and then try again.)

Note: The tools for converting anchor points from corner to smooth will appear in the top left corner after you select an anchor point using the Direct Selection Tool (▶).

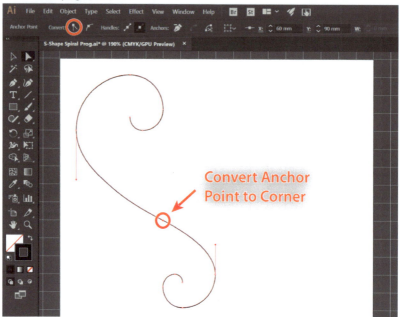

9 After converting the Anchor Point to a straight line, click on the Convert Selected Anchor Points to Smooth button to make a smooth curve between the spirals.

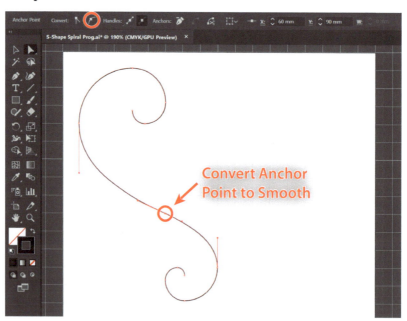

Use the Width Tool to make an interesting spiral design.

Next, we will use the Width Tool to create a spiral shape that has volume.

1   Select the Line Width Tool (▨).

2   Select **View->Snap to Grid** to turn off the Snap to Grid function.

3   Click and drag horizontally on the left most point of the spiral until the width is approximately 10mm.

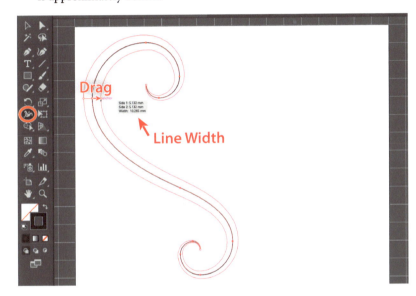

Tip: If the little box showing the line width does not show up, then you probably need to turn off Snap to Grid.

Make sure there is not a checkmark on the menu item:
View->Snap to Grid

4   Click and drag vertically on the top most point of the spiral until the width is approximately 3mm.

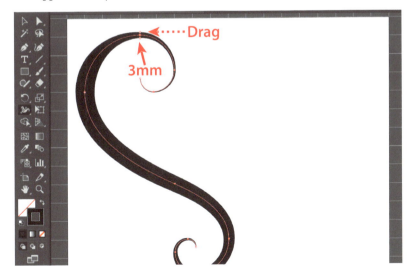

5   Click and drag horizontally on the right most point of the spiral until the
    width is approximately 3mm.

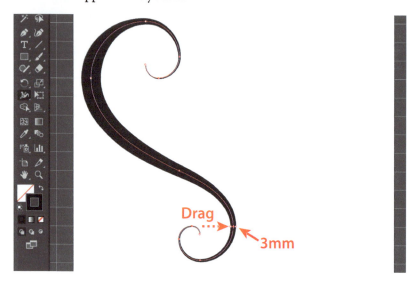

6   Click on the Selection Tool(▶), and select the spiral shape.

7   Select *Object->Path->Outline Stroke* from the top menu bar.

8   Set the fill color to White, the Stroke color to Black and the Stroke Weight to
    1pt.

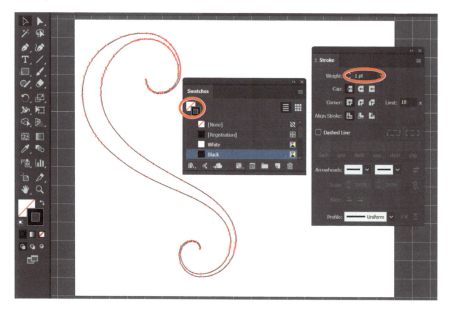

9   Select *Object->Path->Offset Path...* from the top menu bar.

10 In the Offset Path dialogue, set the following:
    Offset: **-2mm**
    Joins: **Miter**
    Miter Limit: **4**

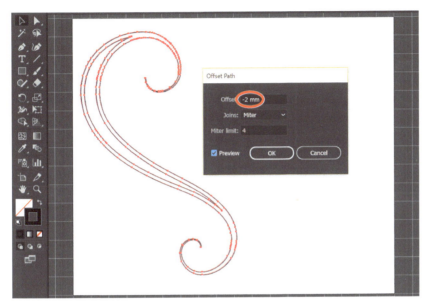

11 Select the crescent shape, and set the Fill Color to Black and the Stroke Color to [None]

Putting it all together...

The following are some example designs that were created by scaling and combining pieces from the previous examples.

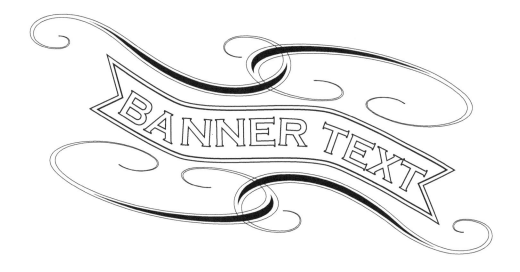

Ornamental Patterns

Complex ornamental patterns are often created simply by repeating basic geometric shapes. With a little experimentation you can quickly generate some intricate designs using the Blend and Pattern functions.

1   Create two objects. They can be lines or shapes.

2   *Select Object->Blend->Blend Options...* from the top menu bar.

3   In the Blend Options dialogue box, set the options you want. If you select "Specified Distance" from the drop-down menu, you can make the objects repeat at an exact distance. *(You are only setting up the options here, so nothing will happen until you do the next step.)*

4   With both objects selected, choose *Object->Blend->Make* from the top menu bar.

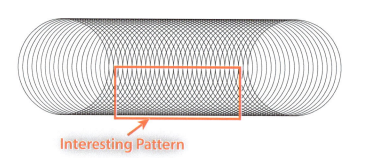

Interesting Pattern

Example 11: Ornamental Border Using Blends

Reduced to show the full page

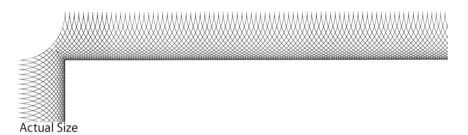

Actual Size

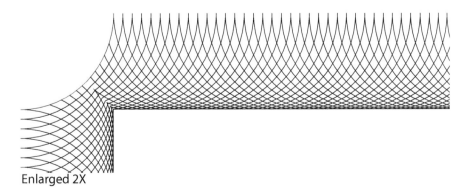

Enlarged 2X

In this example, we will create a complete certificate border using a guilloché pattern. The guilloché pattern for this example will be a simple blend between circles placed in the corners of the page. We will use the same corner circles to clip the border masks as well.

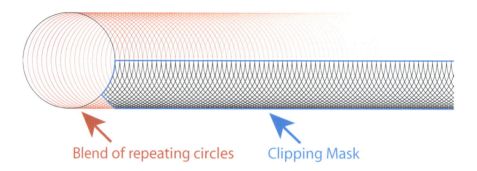

Blend of repeating circles   Clipping Mask

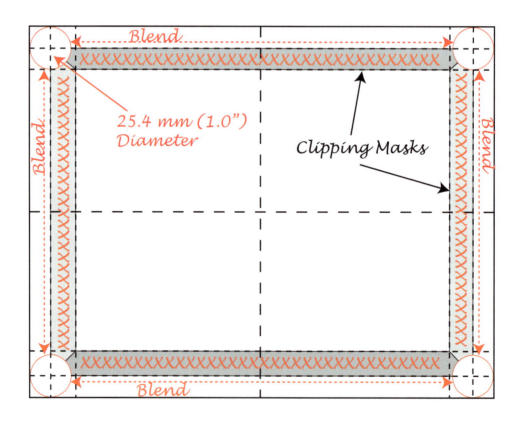

Blend

25.4 mm (1.0")
Diameter

Clipping Masks

Blend

Blend

Blend

Load the Half_Inch_Border_Template

1   Select **File->New from Template**, and then select "EX02 Half Inch Border Template". You can also download the startup file (*EX11 Ornamental Borders Using Blends Start.ai*) from: *DavidTCurtis.wixsite.com/OrnamentalDesign*

2   Verify that the Layers are set up correctly:
     Layers:
             Border
                     Blend Keys
                     Top Border
                     Left Border
                     Bottom Border
                     Right Border
             Guides

Blend Keys

1   Select the Ellipse Tool (⬤). You can find the Ellipse tool by clicking and holding down on the Rectangle Tool.

2   Select the "Blend Keys" sublayer.

3   Click anywhere on the page and the Ellipse Dialogue will appear. Then, set the width and height to 25.4 mm (1.0 inches).

Note: In order to maintain the appearance of spikes along the outer edge of the border, make sure the circles are always twice the height of the final border. Also be sure to position the circles so that the border mask cuts through the center of the circles.

4   Transform the circle to the top left corner using the Transform Panel:

Transform Panel		
Reference Point: *Center*	X: *12.7 mm* Y: *12.7 mm* Rotate: *0°*	W: *25.4 mm* H: *25.4 mm* Shear: *0°*

5   Set the Stroke Weight to 0.25pt, the stroke color to Black and the fill to None.

6   Copy the top left circle.

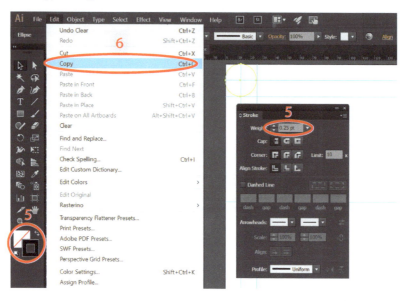

7   Select **Edit->Paste**, and then transform the new circle to the top right corner using the following:

Transform Panel

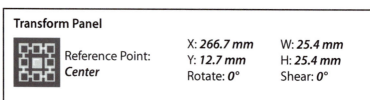

Reference Point:
Center

X: *266.7 mm*   W: *25.4 mm*
Y: *12.7 mm*   H: *25.4 mm*
Rotate: *0°*   Shear: *0°*

8   Paste another circle, and transform the new circle to the bottom left corner using the following:

Transform Panel

Reference Point: *Center*

X: *12.7 mm*   W: *25.4 mm*
Y: *203.2 mm* H: *25.4 mm*
Rotate: *0°*   Shear: *0°*

Tip: You don't have to copy and paste each circle individually. You could copy and paste both top circles and then transform them to the bottom.

9   Paste the last circle, and transform to the bottom right using the following:

Transform Panel

Reference Point: *Center*

X: *266.7 mm* W: *25.4 mm*
Y: *203.2 mm* H: *25.4 mm*
Rotate: *0°*   Shear: *0°*

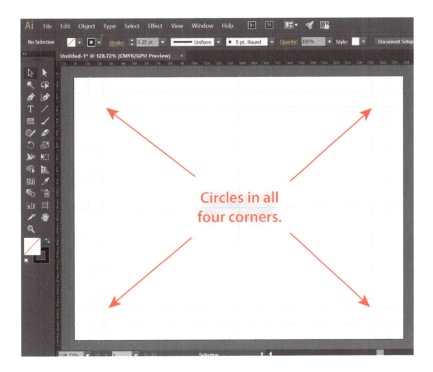

Top Border

1   Copy the top left and top right Blend Keys (circles).

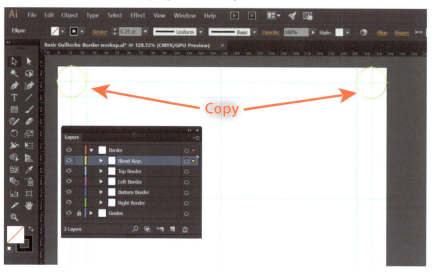

2   Hide the "Blend Keys" sublayer. (*Click on the eye (👁) icon*)

3   Click on the "Top Border" sublayer.

Note: Make sure you use "Paste in Front" so that the circles are placed in front of the border masks. The circles have to be in front in order to be used to cut the corners of the border masks.

4   Select *Edit->Paste in Front*.

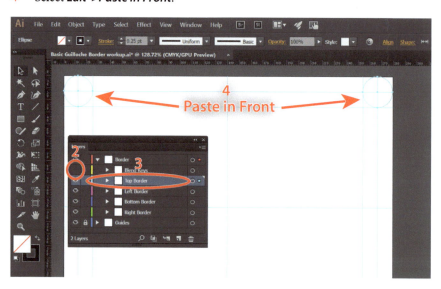

5   Select everything in the "Top Border" sublayer by clicking on the circle to the right of the sublayer name in the Layers Panel. You can also hold down the shift key and click on the Top Border Mask.

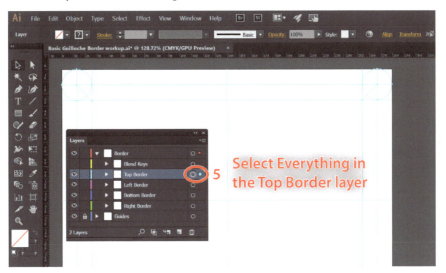

6   Click on the Shape Mode: Minus Front icon in the Pathfinder Panel. You should now have a Top Border Mask with sharp corners now clipped with a semicircle shape.

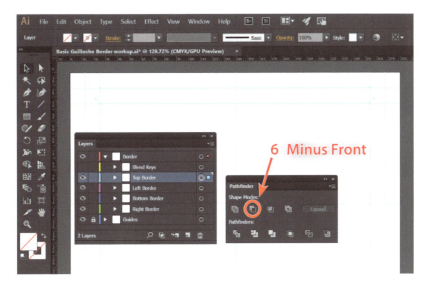

7   Show the "Blend Keys" sublayer, and copy the top left and top right Blend Keys again.

Tip: You do not have to re-copy the circles if you did not copy anything else after copying them the first time.

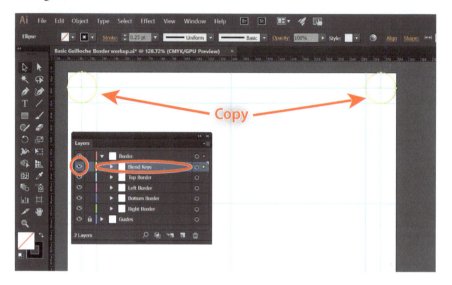

8   Hide the "Blend Keys" sublayer. (*Click on the eye () icon*)

9   Click on the "Top Border" sublayer.

Note: Make sure you use "Paste in Back" so that the circles used to create the blend are placed behind the border mask. The blend has to be behind the mask in order for the clipping mask to work.

10 Select ***Edit->Paste in Back***.

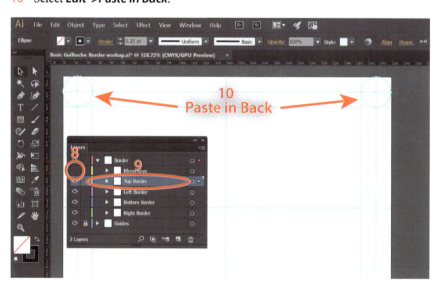

11 Select **Object->Blend->Blend Options**

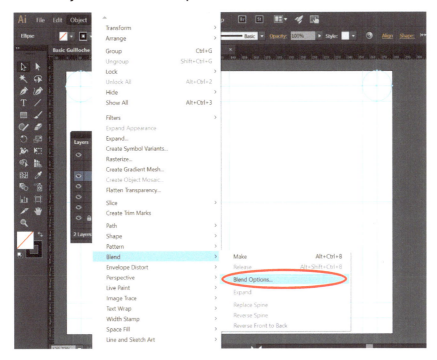

12 In the Blend Options dialog box, change the Spacing option from "Smooth Color" to "Specified Distance".

13 Set the Specified Distance to 1.27 mm (0.05 inches).

14 Make sure the orientation is set to Align to Page.

15 Click on the OK button to create the Top Border blend.

Tip: If you set the blend options before making the blend, those same blend options will be used for each subsequent blend you make.

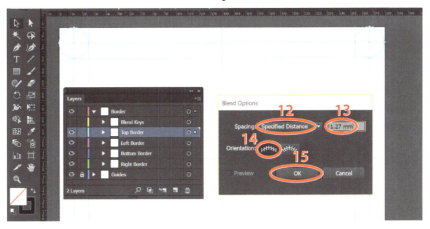

16 Select everything in the "Top Border" sublayer by clicking on the circle to the right of the sublayer name in the Layers Panel.

17 Select *Object->Clipping Mask->Make*.

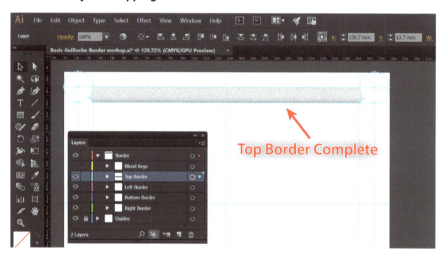

Left Border

1 Hide the "Top Border" sublayer. (*Click on the eye (👁) icon*)

2 Show the "Blend Keys" sublayer. (*Click on the space for the eye (👁) icon*)

3 Copy the top left and bottom left Blend Keys (circles).

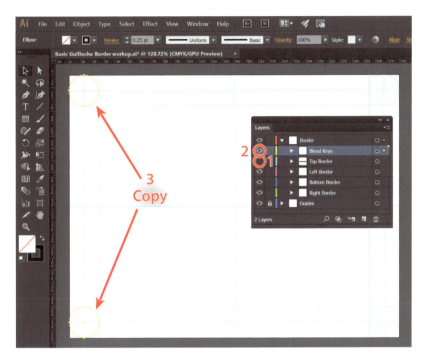

4   Hide the "Blend Keys" sublayer. (*Click on the eye* (👁) *icon*)

5   Click on the "Left Border" sublayer.

6   Select *Edit->Paste in Front*.

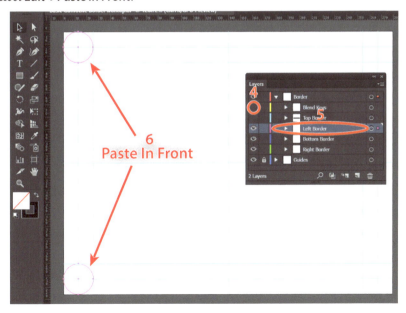

7   Select everything in the "Left Border" sublayer by clicking on the circle to the right of the sublayer name in the Layers Panel.

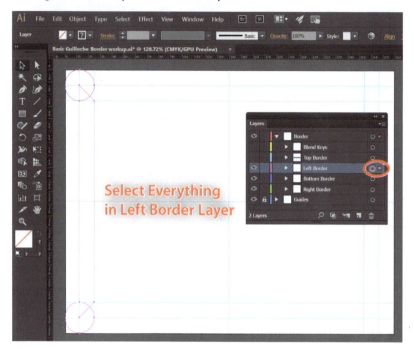

8   Click on the Shape Mode: Minus Front icon in the Pathfinder Panel. You should now have a Left Border Mask with sharp corners now clipped with a semicircle shape.

9   Show the "Blend Keys" sublayer, and copy the top left and bottom left Blend
    Keys again.

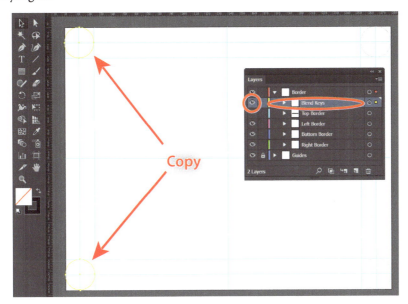

10 Hide the "Blend Keys" sublayer.

11 Click on the "Left Border" sublayer.

12 Select *Edit->Paste in Back*.

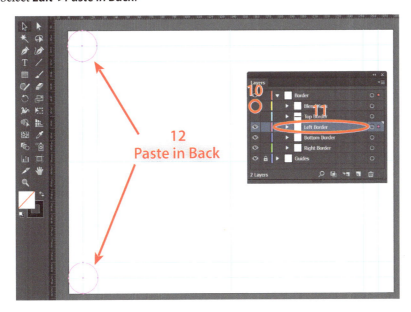

13 Select **Object->Blend->Make**. (If the blend does not look right, select ***Object->Blend->Blend*** Options and make sure the blend options are set the same as the top border.)

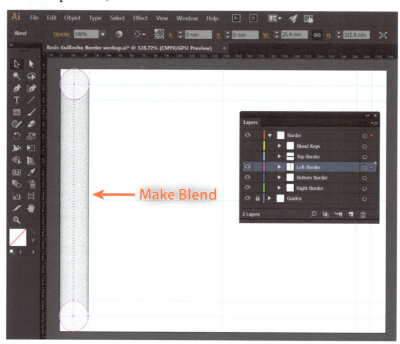

14 Select everything in the "Left Border" sublayer by clicking on the circle to the right of the sublayer name in the Layers Panel.

15   Select *Object->Clipping Mask->Make*.

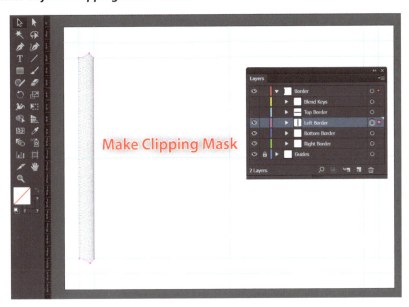

Bottom Border

1   Hide the "Left Border" sublayer.

2   Show the "Blend Keys" sublayer.

3   Copy the bottom left and bottom right Blend Keys (circles).

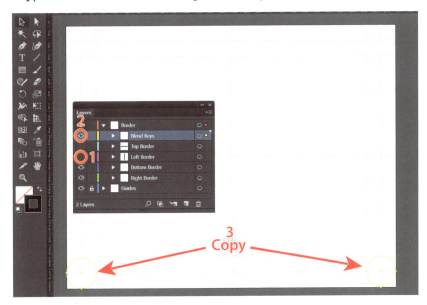

4 Hide the "Blend Keys" sublayer.

5 Click on the "Bottom Border" sublayer.

6 Select *Edit->Paste in Front*.

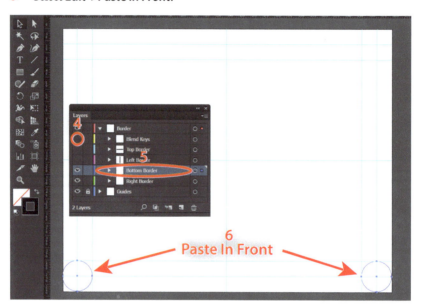

7 Select everything in the "Bottom Border" sublayer by clicking on the circle to the right of the sublayer name in the Layers Panel.

8   Click on the Shape Mode: Minus Front icon in the Pathfinder Panel. You should now have a Bottom Border Mask with sharp corners now clipped with a semicircle shape.

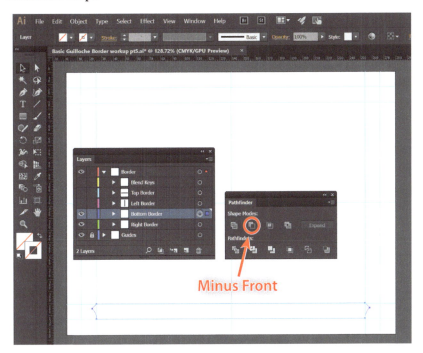

9   Show the "Blend Keys" sublayer, and copy the bottom left and bottom right Blend Keys again.

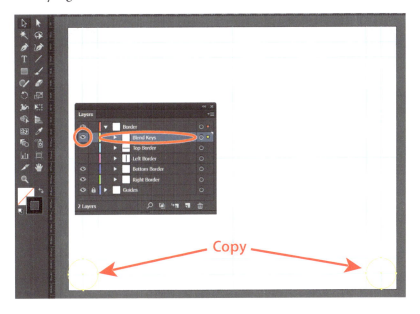

10   Hide the "Blend Keys" sublayer.

11   Click on the "Bottom Border" sublayer.

12   Select *Edit->Paste in Back*.

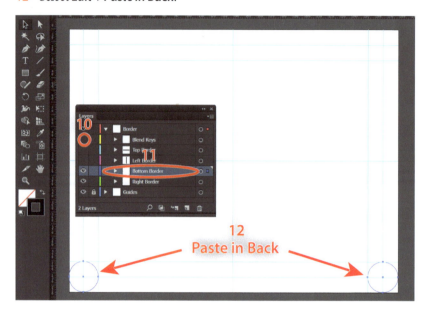

13   Select *Object->Blend->Make*. (If the blend does not look right, select *Object->Blend->Blend Options* and make sure the blend options are set the same as the top border.)

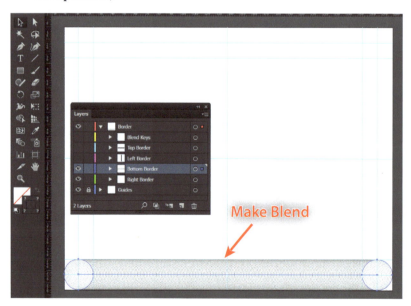

14 Select everything in the "Bottom Border" sublayer by clicking on the circle to the right of the sublayer name in the Layers Panel.

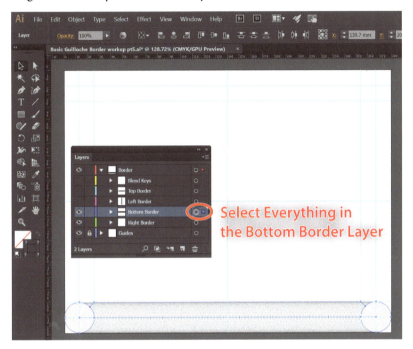

15 Select *Object->Clipping Mask->Make*.

Right Border

1   Hide the "Bottom Border" sublayer.

2   Show the "Blend Keys" sublayer.

3   Copy the top right and bottom right Blend Keys (circles).

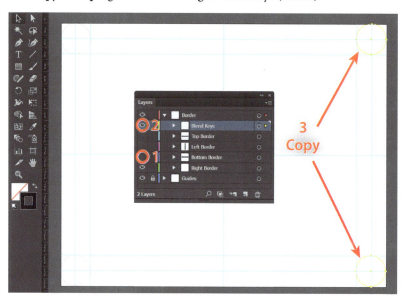

4   Hide the "Blend Keys" sublayer.

5   Click on the "Right Border" sublayer.

6   Select *Edit->Paste in Front*.

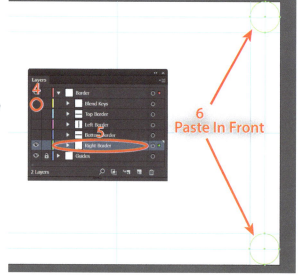

7   Select everything in the "Right Border" sublayer by clicking on the circle to the right of the sublayer name in the Layers Panel.

8   Click on the Shape Mode: Minus Front icon in the Pathfinder Panel. You should now have a Right Border Mask with sharp corners now clipped with a semicircle shape.

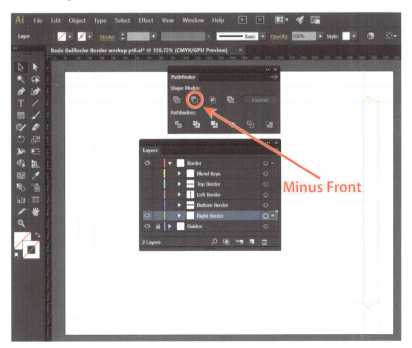

9   Show the "Blend Keys" sublayer, and copy the top right and bottom right Blend Keys again.

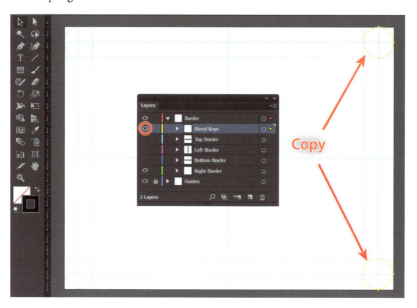

10   Hide the "Blend Keys" sublayer.

11   Click on the "Right Border" sublayer.

12   Select *Edit->Paste in Back*.

13 Select **Object->Blend->Make**. (If the blend does not look right, select **Object->Blend->Blend Options** and make sure the blend options are set the same as the top border.)

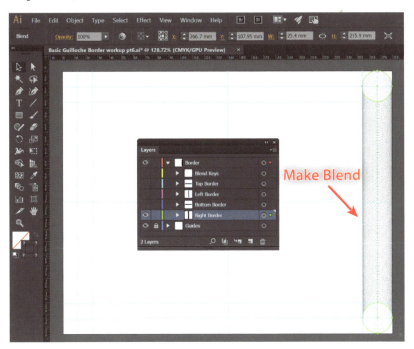

14 Select everything in the "Right Border" sublayer by clicking on the circle to the right of the sublayer name in the Layers Panel.

15   Select *Object->Clipping Mask->Make*.

16   Show all of the border sublayers, and you are finished.

Note: Before sending your designs out for printing or publication, you will need to delete extra layers like the "Blend Keys" layer in this example. Be sure to save a "working" copy with the extra layers also, just in case you want to make modifications later.

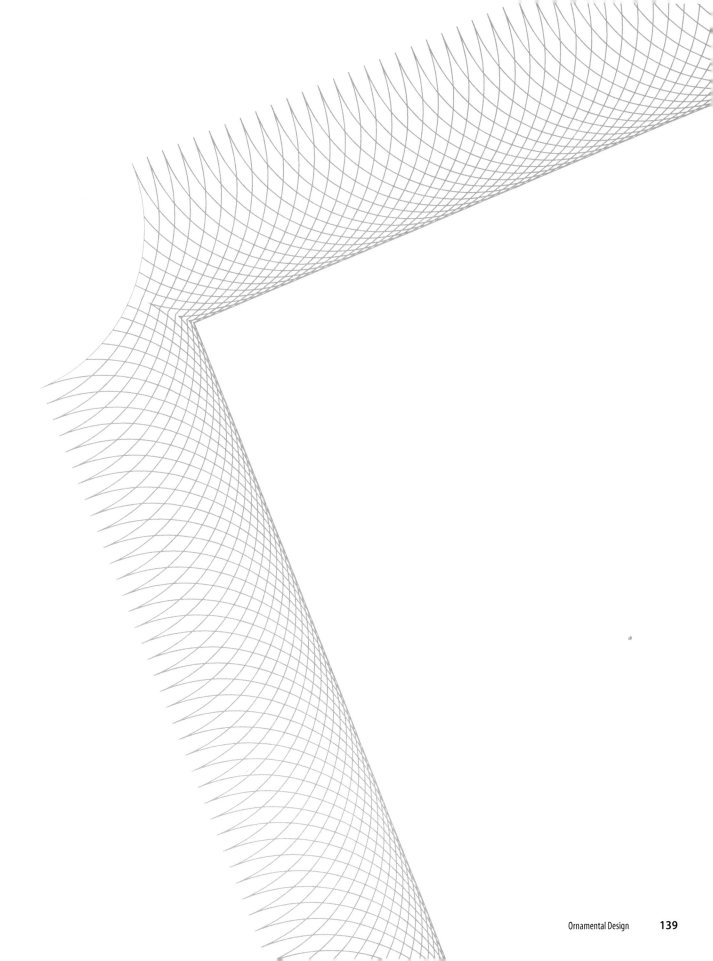

What If We Replace the Circle With a Different Shape?

The following are samples of replacing the circle shape in the previous example.

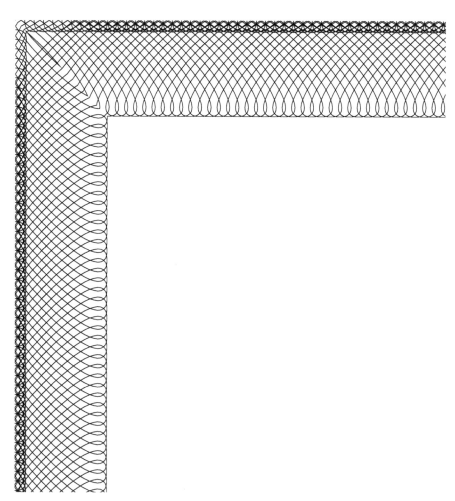

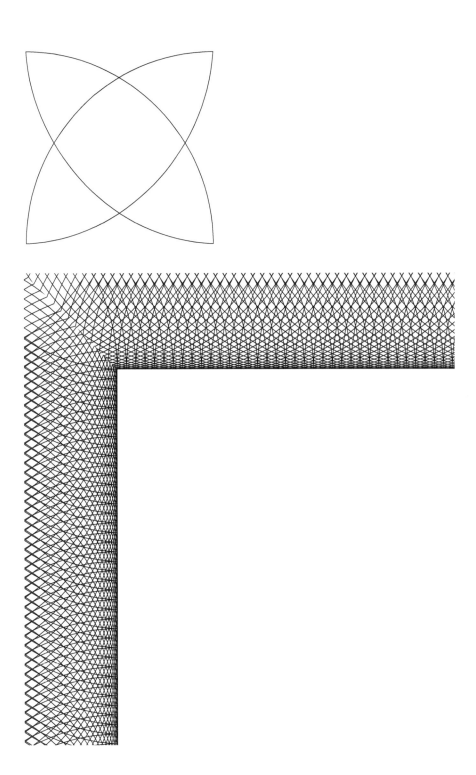

EXAMPLE 12: Ornamental Border Using a Pattern

The following is an example of how to create a pattern that can be applied to any enclosed shape. This method is basically just a simple blend between two oval shapes that repeats and overlaps.

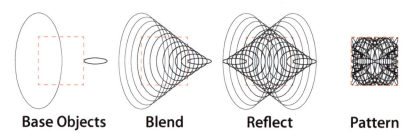

Base Objects   **Blend**   **Reflect**   **Pattern**

File Setup

First, we will setup a new document with a letter size page.

1   Select *File->New...* from the top menu bar. You can also download the startup file (*EX12 Ornamental Borders Using Pattern Start.ai*) from: *DavidTCurtis.wixsite.com/OrnamentalDesign*

2   In the New Document Dialogue use the following settings:
Name:
Ex12 Guilloche Pattern
Number of Artboards: **1**
Size: **Letter**
Units: **Millimeters**
Width: **279.4 mm**
Height: **215.9 mm**
Orientation: **Landscape** (Horizontal)
Bleed: **0 mm** (for all four options: Top, Bottom…)
Color Mode: **CMYK**
Raster Effects: **High (300ppi)**
Preview Mode: **Default**

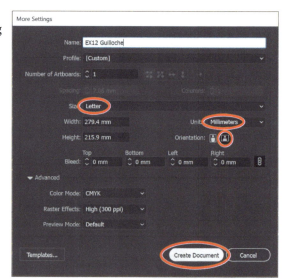

3   Select *View->Fit Artboard in Window* from the top menu bar.

4   In the Layers panel, change the name of "Layer 1" to "Guides". (Double-click on the layer name to change the text.)

5   Select **View->Rulers->Show Rulers** from the top menu bar.

6   Click down on the left ruler and drag across a guide. Use the Transform panel to position the guide as follows:

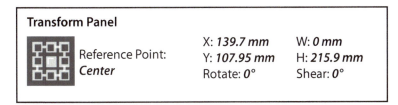

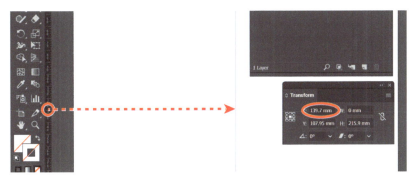

7   Click down on the top ruler and drag down another guide. Use the Transform panel to position the guide as follows:

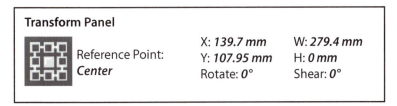

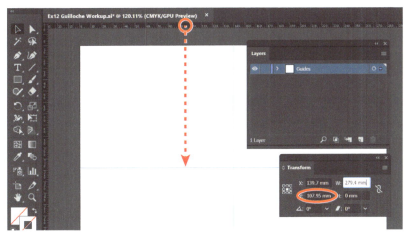

8   Lock the "Guides" layer.

9   Create a new layer.

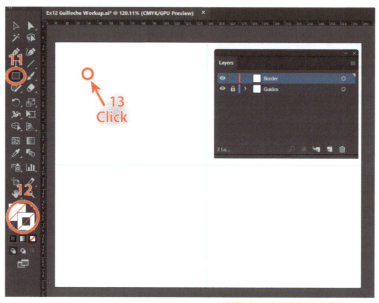

10   Name the new layer "Border".

11   Select the Rectangle Tool (▢).

12   Set the Fill and Stroke to [None].

13   Make sure the "Border" layer is selected and click anywhere on the page.

14   In the rectangle dialogue box, enter:
     Width: **254.0 mm**
     Height: **190.5 mm**
     Click the "OK" button.

15   With the rectangle selected, use the Transform Panel to position the top left
     corner of the rectangle 12.7 mm (1/2 inch) from the top left of the page.

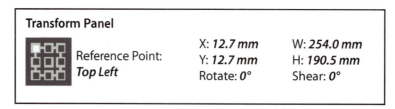

Transform Panel			
Reference Point: *Top Left*	X: *12.7 mm* Y: *12.7 mm* Rotate: *0°*	W: *254.0 mm* H: *190.5 mm* Shear: *0°*	

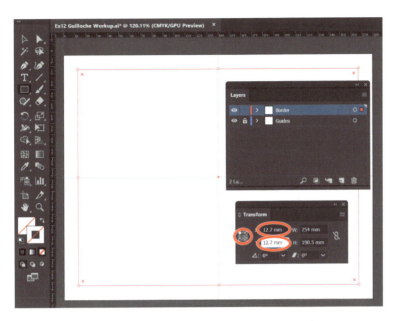

16   Select *Object->Path->Offset Path...* from the top menu bar.

17   In the Offset Path dialogue enter the following:
Offset: **-12.7 mm**
Joins: **Miter**
Miter limit: **4**
Select the "OK" button

18   Select both rectangles using the Selection Tool (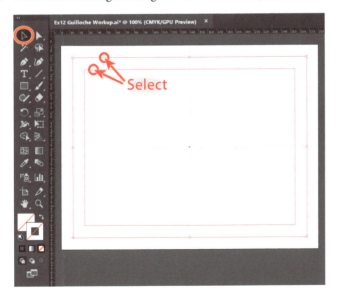).

Tip: There are several ways to select multiple objects. If you are using the selection tool (🔺), click on the first object, then hold down the <shift> key and click on other objects to add them to the selection.

Another way is to click and drag in a diagonal direction to form a box around the objects you want to select.

You can also use one of the selection tools like the Magic Wand or Lasso Tool.

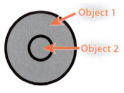

19 **Select Object->Compound Path->Make** from the top menu bar. The two
rectangles should now be one object.

20 Set the Stroke Weight to 0.5pt and the Stroke Color to Black.

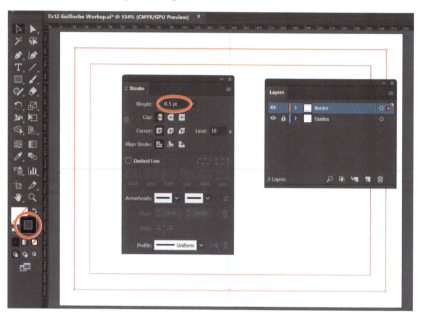

21 Hide the "Border Mask" layer.

Pattern Workup
Next, we will create the guilloché pattern.

1 Create a new layer.

2 Name the new layer: "Pattern Workup".

3   Move the origin to the center of the page.

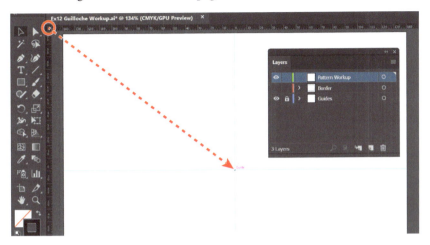

4   Select the Rectangle Tool (▢).

5   Set Fill and Stroke to [None].

6   Click somewhere near the center of the page

7   Enter the following into the Rectangle dialogue box:
    Width: **12.7 mm**
    Height: **12.7 mm**
    Select the "OK" button.

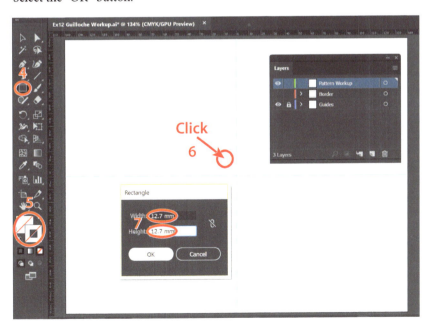

8   With the rectangle selected, use the Transform Panel to position the rectangle in the center of the page.

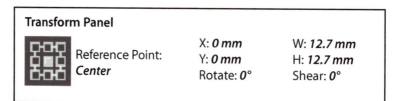

10   Select the Ellipse Tool (⬭), and click somewhere near the center of the page.

9   Zoom in on the rectangle like shown below:

Tip: There are several ways to zoom in on an object. You can select the zoom tool (🔍) and click on the object several times until it fills the screen. You can also click and drag a rectangle around the object. Another way is to hold down the <Command> key (Mac) or the <Ctrl> key (Windows), and then press the plus or minus keys to zoom in or out.

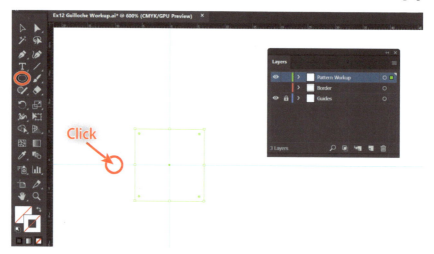

11 Enter the following into the Ellipse dialogue:
Width: **12.7 mm**
Height: **25.4 mm**
Select the "OK" button.

12 Use the Transform panel to position the oval as follows:
X: **-6.35 mm**
Y: **0 mm**

Transform Panel

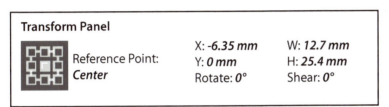

Reference Point: **Center**	X: *-6.35 mm* Y: *0 mm* Rotate: *0°*	W: *12.7 mm* H: *25.4 mm* Shear: *0°*

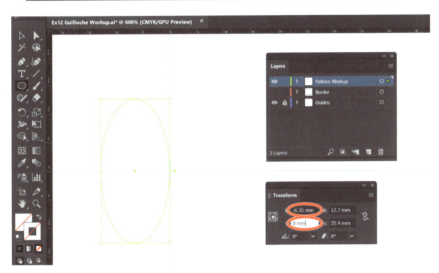

13 Set the Stroke Width to 0.25pt and the Stroke Color to Black

14 Make sure the Ellipse Tool (⬤) is still selected, and click somewhere near the center of the page again.

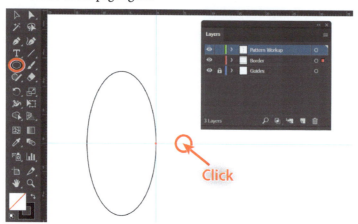

15 Enter the following into the Ellipse dialogue:
Width: **6.35 mm**
Height: **1.57 mm**
Select the "OK" button.

16 Use the Transform panel to position the oval as follows:
X: **9.53 mm**
Y: **0 mm**

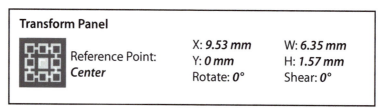

Transform Panel

	Reference Point: *Center*	X: *9.53 mm*	W: *6.35 mm*
		Y: *0 mm*	H: *1.57 mm*
		Rotate: *0°*	Shear: *0°*

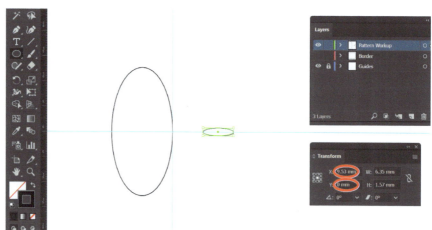

17 Set the Stroke Width to 0.5pt and the Stroke Color to Black

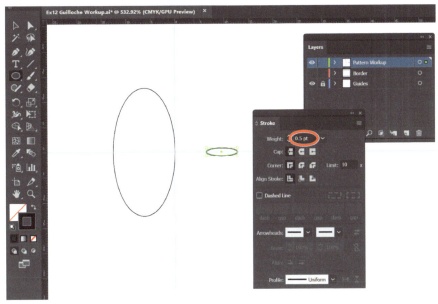

18 Select both ovals using the Selection Tool (▶).

19 Select **Object->Blend->Blend Options...** from the top menu bar.

20 In the Blend Options dialogue box enter the following:
Spacing: **Specified Steps 10**
Orientation: **Align to Page**
Select the "OK" button

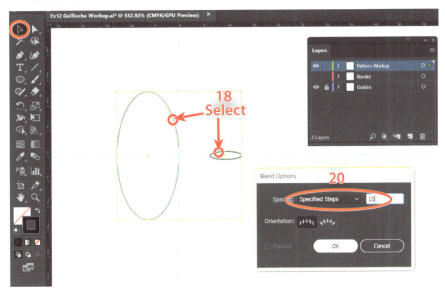

21 Select **Object->Blend->Make** from the top menu bar.

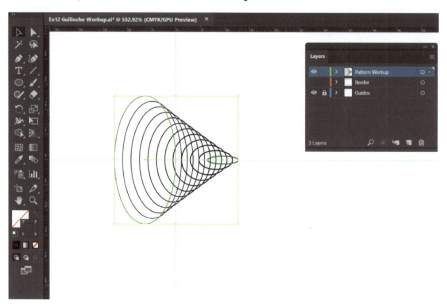

22 Select **Object->Transform->Reflect** from the top menu bar.

23 In the Reflect dialogue box, enter the following:
Axis: **Vertical**
Select the "**Copy**" button

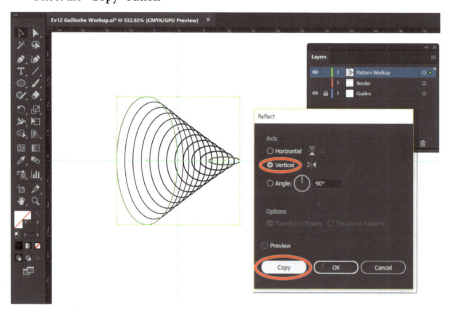

24 Select everything in the "Border" layer by clicking on the circle next to the layer name in the layers panel. *(Both blend objects and the 12.7mm square should be selected.)*

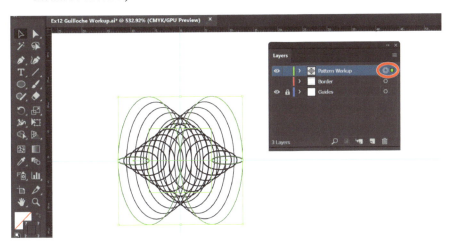

25 Select **Object->Pattern->Make** from the top menu bar.

26 In the Pattern Options panel enter the following:
    Name: **Guilloche Pattern**

27 Select "Done" at the top of the pattern preview page

Tip: The repeat width and height of this pattern is based on the 12.7mm square we created in steps 4-7. In the Patten Options dialogue, you can change the 12.7mm width and height to see how it affects the pattern.

Applying the Pattern

Next, we will fill the border with the guilloché pattern.

1   **Select View->Fit Artboard in Window** from the top menu bar.

2   In the Layers Panel, hide the "Pattern Workup" layer.

3   Show the "Border Mask" layer.

4   Select the border mask object (rectangle shape).

5   Open the Swatches panel.

6   Set the Fill to the swatch labeled "Guilloche Pattern".

Note: If you move an object with a fill pattern, the pattern will stay stationary and not move with the object. To make the pattern move with the object, select: **Object->Expand...**

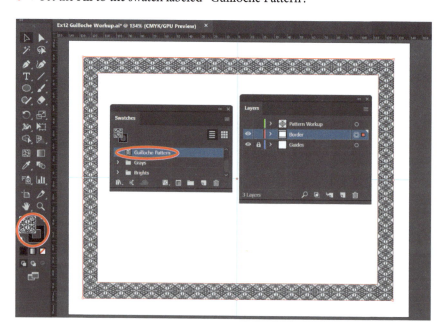

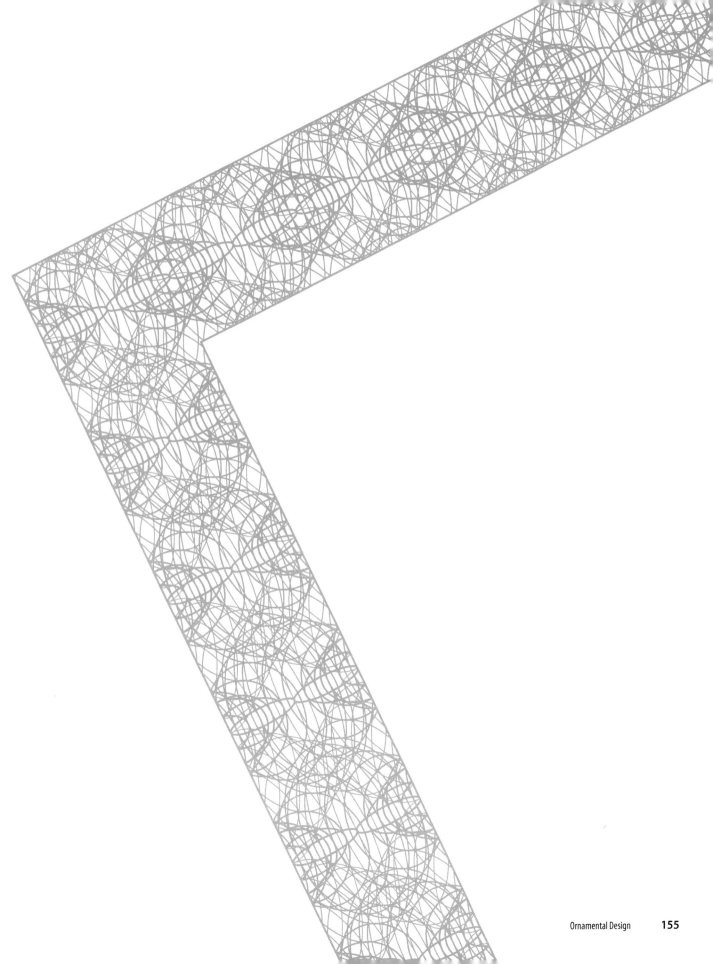

About the Author

David T. Curtis works for the United States Treasury Department, Bureau of Engraving and Printing, Product Design Division responsible for designing United States currency, passports and other security documents. He has been designing with Adobe Illustrator for over 25 years.

David got his start in computer graphics at a young age in the early nineteen eighties, when computers were just starting to become common place in homes across America. His father brought home a European Sinclair ZX81 computer, but David was not too excited about it at first. He told his father, "Dad, I want an Atari so I can play video games." His father replied, "But son, with this computer, you can make your own video games." This was the inspiration for David to get started with graphics and imaging. A few years later, he went on to win a film competition with his trusty Commodore 64 computer. He earned a computer graphics art degree from the University of Maryland, and went to work for the Printing Corporation of America. David worked in the commercial printing industry for many years and then was hired by the United States Treasury Department to develop and enhance technology for new United States currency designs. David has received multiple technical achievement awards, and is a recognized technical expert worldwide.